I am so excited and thrilled by the unexpected pleasure of knowing that the unique life of William Carey Strother is being explored and celebrated in book form! In my continuing research on the films and life of Harold Lloyd, I have long known Strother's importance in inspiring arguably Lloyd's most famed film, Safety Last! *Bill Strother's human spider histrionics made him a legion of fans—and now, through the Herculean efforts of Donna Strother Deekens, admirers will learn that there was life after* Safety Last! *And what a life it was! This book is the most precious of all commodities—original research conducted with love—and though I am sure the climb was arduous, the result is so worth the work. This is true biographical archaeology you are holding—filled with dust, discoveries, exasperation and exhilaration—and I say "Congratulations" to Donna and "Way to go, buddy" to Bill!*

ANNETTE D'AGOSTINO LLOYD
Author, *The Harold Lloyd Encyclopedia*

THE REAL SANTA OF

Miller & Rhoads

THE EXTRAORDINARY LIFE OF BILL STROTHER

DONNA STROTHER DEEKENS

Foreword by Phillip L. Wenz

THE
History
PRESS

Published by The History Press
Charleston, SC 29403
www.historypress.net

Front cover: Santa Bill Strother at Miller & Rhoads posed for the December 22, 1951 issue of the *Saturday Evening Post*. *Bill Strother cover photograph ©SEPS licensed by Curtis Licensing, Indianapolis, Indiana. All rights reserved.* *Back cover, top left*: A color vintage postcard featuring the Human Spider climbing the McAllister Hotel in Miami, Florida, circa 1919. *Courtesy foundimage.com*; *top right*: Bill Strother is pictured in the *Calgary Daily Herald* climbing the Herald Building in Calgary, Canada, September 23, 1921. *Dr. Donald Smith Private Collection*; *bottom*: Bill Strother just before he climbed the Hibernia Bank Building in New Orleans on April 22, 1919. Here he implores a large gathering to buy Victory Bonds. *Photo by John T. Mendes ©The Historic New Orleans Collection, Gift of Waldemar S. Nelson, Acc. No. 2003.0182.193.*

First published 2014
Second printing 2015

ISBN 9781540211606

Library of Congress Cataloging-in-Publication Data

Deekens, Donna Strother.
The real Santa of Miller & Rhoads : the extraordinary life of Bill Strother / Donna Strother Deekens.
pages cm
Summary: "Discover the fascinating life of Bill Strother, the celebrated 'real' Santa at Miller & Rhoads in Richmond, Virginia"-- Provided by publisher.
Includes bibliographical references and index.
ISBN 978-1-62619-696-4 (paperback)
1. Strother, Bill, 1896-1957. 2. Department store Santas--Virginia--Richmond--Biography. 3. Miller & Rhoads--Employees--Biography. 4. Miller & Rhoads--History--20th century. 5. Stunt performers--United States--Biography. 6. Buildering--United States--History--20th century. I. Title. II. Title: Real Santa of Miller and Rhoads.
HF5465.U64M5527 2014
394.2663--dc23
[B]
2014033885

To the loving and inestimable giving spirit of Santa Claus Bill Strother, whose genius, innovation, compassion and devotion to all his roles in life, but especially his "Real Santa," endeared him to the hearts of everyone who delighted in his "magic," and who, because of him, still believe!

Alas! How dreary the world would be if there was no Santa Claus!...There would be no childlike faith then, no poetry, no romance to make tolerable this existence.
—*Francis P. Church, "Yes, Virginia, There Is a Santa Claus,"* New York Sun, *September 21, 1897*

CONTENTS

Foreword, by Phillip L. Wenz   11
Acknowledgements   17
Introduction. "I Believe!"   19

I. SETTING "HIGH" STANDARDS
1. Young Carey   31
2. Hanging Out: "Buildering"   39
3. "'Will You Walk Into My Parlor?' Said the Spider to the Fly…"   43
4. Climbing for the War Effort…and Beyond   57
5. "O Canada!": A Thrill Ride for Our Neighbor to the North   81
6. Climbing Toward an Unexpected Hollywood Moment   89
7. Falling in Love…but Able to Leap Tall Buildings No More!   103
8. "Buddy, Can You Spare a Dime?"   107
9. Heading "Back East"   109

II. "SANTA MAGIC!"
10. The Man Who Would Be Santa Claus   113
11. End of an Era, but the Tradition Lives On   179

Album of the Real Santa of Miller & Rhoads,
    Santa Bill Strother and Children of Yesteryear   185
Notes   199
About the Author   205

FOREWORD

BY PHILLIP L. WENZ

S ometimes life imitates art, but in the case of Bill Strother, his life became a canvas of unique experiences where he created the art. He was a man with many, many aspirations. The only way to understand him is to compare his endeavors to the layers of an onion. As with the onion, Strother had many layers, and when you peel them away, you can find the heart of the man who brought so much happiness and entertainment to hundreds of thousands of people of all ages.

Strother was born in 1896, just before the turn of the twentieth century and the era of new prosperity, inventions and entertainment. As a son of the state of North Carolina, he was raised with good moral values and the desire to serve others. One can only imagine the events that inspired a young Bill Strother and that would lead him on his many adventures as an adult.

A man with many hats, Strother was a salesman, innkeeper and cook, among his many occupations. But it was two of his most unusual callings that would leave a lasting impression on those who saw him or learned about him years later. These two pursuits—climbing buildings as the "Human Spider" and the role of Santa Claus at Miller & Rhoads Department Store in Richmond, Virginia—would make Strother an American icon.

As the "Human Spider," Strother gained prominence in many areas and cities in North America. Many of the buildings he climbed were some of the best-known skyscrapers of the day in major cities such as New York, Chicago, Los Angeles, Toronto and Montreal. Strother used these stunts to help many local charities. These climbing feats caught the attention of

Hollywood and were the basis for the silent-era movie *Safety Last!* starring Harold Lloyd.

Strother's career as the "Real" Santa Claus at Miller & Rhoads department store began in 1942. It would be a role he would come to treasure for fifteen years. As Santa, Strother developed a unique perspective on the character and used all his experiences to make Santa come to life like very few before or since have done. His contributions to the Santa vocation, especially in Virginia, are still used as a guide for many to this day.

I first discovered Bill Strother while doing research on Santa history while I was still in high school. I found a book in the school library called *All About Christmas*, which had a chapter about Santa Claus. In this chapter, there was a mention of the "World's Highest Paid Santa Claus" and his magnificent beard, eyebrows and mustache. His name was Bill Strother.

With the lead of the "World's Highest Paid Santa Claus," I found the commentary listed in the Reader's Guide and soon had the magazine article in front of me. I marveled at the story and its content about this man. Bill Strother would soon become a researched "Santa mentor" to me.

Gathering as much information as I could about Strother, I soon learned that his interpretation of Santa Claus was rather unique among the Santas of the golden age of department store Kris Kringles. He developed and established traditions at Miller & Rhoads that are treasured memories to thousands and are continued to this day by his successors. Strother's Santa Claus became the "Real" Santa Claus.

Instead of just talking to the children with all the basic questions and patter, Strother took Santa to a level that included pure performance art, which became a show for all who witnessed his appearances. As Santa, Strother had the look, the acting and improvisational skills and a great sense of showmanship that captured the imaginations of both children and adults.

For more than a decade, tens of thousands would flock each Christmas to downtown Richmond to see the "Real" Santa Claus. They enjoyed seeing Santa enter the "Santa setup" through the chimney. They saw him comb his beard and place his hat on the back of the Santa throne. At lunchtime in the great Tea Room, they saw Santa drink his milk and help serve the delicious "Rudolph" cake to all. They saw the "Real" Santa who was a true "man of the people."

After learning as much as I could about Strother, I realized that his use of performance art was something that should be included in my rendition of Santa Claus. Becoming a complete Santa was my goal. I wanted and

A proud mom and her fun-loving son visit with the Real Santa of Miller & Rhoads, Bill Strother, at the store, circa 1948. *Photo by William Edwin Booth, courtesy Virginia Historical Society.*

eventually acquired the skill of improvisational performance art that helped me grow as a professional Santa Claus. And I have Bill Strother to thank for that.

Today, Bill Strother stands among the best ever to have worn the red suit, and his career is legendary. He is the most famous Santa in the history of Virginia and is a charter member of the International Santa

Bill Strother
"Miller & Rhoads Legendary Santa Claus"
Richmond, Virginia
1896-1957

Santa Claus Hall of Fame
Charter Member-December 22, 2010

Miller & Rhoads Department Store hired former Hollywood stunt man Bill Strother to fill Santa's big red suit in 1942. Strother brought with him many techniques from Hollywood and made the Miller & Rhoads Santa Claus a symbol of the Christmas season. His makeup, designed by the famous Max Factor, took Strother about two hours to put on, and he was, without a doubt, the most realistic Santa Claus ever seen. In addition, he devised a special Santa act. After appearing out of a chimney, he received children on his lap and by use of a concealed throat-mike on an assistant, was able to address each child by name. No act at any theater in Richmond ever drew the crowds, adults as well as children, that flocked to see this Santa Claus appear out of a chimney. Bill Strother not only became the most famous Santa Claus in the history of Virginia, he was also the world's highest paid Santa Claus according to an article in the Saturday Evening Post in 1951.

Above: The Candy Castle opened in 1935 in Santa Claus, Indiana, and is the home of the International Santa Claus Hall of Fame. *Phillip L. Wenz Private Collection.*

Left: Santa Bill Strother was one of the fourteen charter members inducted into the International Hall of Fame in 2010. A plaque in his honor hangs in the Candy Castle's "Round Room." *Phillip L. Wenz Private Collection.*

Claus Hall of Fame in Santa Claus, Indiana. But most importantly, Bill Strother will always be the "Real" Santa to those who were fortunate enough to sit on his knee and whisper to him their Christmas wishes, hopes and dreams.

About Phillip L. Wenz

If ever there was a man born to be Santa Claus, it is Phillip L. Wenz. As a four-year-old child, he donned his first Santa outfit. By the time he was fourteen, he was in his first parade, and at the ripe old age of twenty-three, he became the year-round Santa Claus for the iconic Santa's Village theme park in Dundee, Illinois. It is an association he has now had for nearly thirty years. He is the longest tenured Santa in the park's fifty-five-year history and is one of the very few true full-time year-round professional Santa Clauses in history. He appears in costume at the park and at special events over two hundred days each year.

Wenz has appeared in over forty Christmas parades, including the nationally televised parades in Chicago, Illinois, and Houston, Texas. He has been Santa on numerous TV shows, billboards, commercials and magazine covers, along with appearing at some of the nation's largest corporate and civic holiday events, including emceeing the Christmas tree lighting ceremonies in both Chicago and Houston. He has been given the title of "Chicago's Very Own Santa" by WGN-TV, awarded the 1994 Brass Ring Award for Best Theme Park Commercial by the International Association of Amusement Parks and Attractions (IAAPA) and received the "Hats Off 2 Houston" award from KPRC-TV in Houston. In 2012, he was presented the "Spirit of St. Nicholas" award in Detroit, Michigan.

His résumé also includes work in Santa Claus, Indiana, at the historic Candy Castle; consulting on Christmas programs; and being a published author. He is considered a leading authority and historian on the Santa Claus legend, history and folklore. Wenz is, bar none, one of the most experienced Santas ever and is the creator of the Santa Claus Oath, which is widely accepted by nearly every Santa portrayer across the globe.

In December 2010, Wenz was bestowed with the highest honor a Santa Claus can receive: enshrinement as a charter member into the International Santa Claus Hall of Fame in Santa Claus, Indiana. Of the original fourteen honorees, including the first department store Santa and several men born in the nineteenth century, Wenz was the first living Santa to be inducted. He was also recognized by his peers from the Santa Claus community in March 2013 when he received the first ever "Legendary Santa Claus" award.

The Santa Claus Oath

I will seek knowledge to be well versed in the mysteries of bringing Christmas cheer and good will to all the people that I encounter in my journeys and travels.
I shall be dedicated to hearing the secret dreams of both children and adults.
I understand that the true and only gift I can give, as Santa, is myself.
I acknowledge that some of the requests I will hear will be difficult and sad.
I know in these difficulties there lies an opportunity to bring a spirit of warmth, understanding and compassion.
I know the "real reason for the season" and know that I am blessed to be able to be a part of it.
I realize that I belong to a brotherhood and will be supportive, honest and show fellowship to my peers.
I promise to use "my" powers to create happiness, spread love and make fantasies come to life in the true and sincere tradition of the Santa Claus Legend.
I pledge myself to these principles as a descendant of St. Nicholas, the gift giver of Myra.

ACKNOWLEDGEMENTS

I am indebted to many people for this biography about Bill Strother. Among them are Banks Smither; Phillip Wenz and the International Santa Claus Hall of Fame; Annette D'Agostino Lloyd; John Bengtson; Suzanne Lloyd, Liz Jobson and Sara Juarez of Harold Lloyd Entertainment, Inc.; Dr. Donald B. Smith; Michael Futch; Harry Sanders; Will Robinson and Megan Proctor of the Wilson County Public Libraries, Wilson and Stantonsburg, North Carolina; Fambrough Brownlee and Molly Rawls of the Forsyth County Public Library, Winston-Salem, North Carolina; Dan and Marguerite Whitley; Roger Bynum; Penn Burke; Bertha Burke; Lewis Parks; Sue Ferrell; Carolyn Drudge; Joe and Sally Pace; Tom Mitchell; Nelson and Marilyn Strother; Robin Dean; Kim Anderson and Steve Case of the State Archives of North Carolina, Raleigh, North Carolina; George and Carol Bryson; Bill Martin, Meg Hughes and Kelly Kerney of the Valentine Richmond History Center; Heather Beattie and Jamison Davis of the Virginia Historical Society; Mary Lou Eichhorn of the John T. Mendes Photography Collection of the Historic New Orleans Collection; Cris Pinquinela of Curtis Publishing, Inc.; Chronicling America of the Library of Congress; Sarah Lind and Wendy Weig of the Felix Adler Children's Discovery Center, Clinton, Iowa; Clyde Nordan; Tim O' Gorman; Judy and Ron Jones; Wayne and Lynne Tatum; Linda Scott; Nancy Emerson; Doug and Sandy Riddell; Colleen Simmons; Cathy and Curtis Miller; Nancy and Al Dorin; Lyn Presson; Katharine Townsend; Marshall Knox; Jim Knox; Connie Burton; Frances Broaddus-Crutchfield; Kathy Brooks; Donna and

Carter Hudgins; Dennis and Judy Wrenn; Janet Ralston; Rick Pearman; Leckie Conners; Jane Osborne Johnson; Martha Watts; Don Dale; Tom and Dottie Mears; Gail Brookings; Joan and Bill Barns; Brent Deekens; Greg Deekens; Josh Yeager; Fred Harris; Jane Westbrook; Lamar Brandt; Jean Duke; John Jackson of VT Special Collections; John Whitting; Howie Hoffman; David Castle, Charlie Nuckols; Wes Nuckols; Tom Long; Dale Parris; Tim Connaghan; Lee Milstead; Michael J. Rielly; Wayne Dementi; Jody Weaver Yuhase; Monk Moore; Michael Jones; Amy Jones; Kathy and Andy Deekens; Anne Deekens; Vaughan Gary; Rick Smith; Earl and Ann Palmer Roth; Hank and Millie Loughridge; Darcy Mahan; Jan McCormack; Martha Steger; Memory Box Archives; Cate Bell of Found Image; Marc Wanamaker of Bison Archives; Dorothy Juergens of Hometown Vintage; Historic Images; Virginia Chamber of Commerce; Dementi Studios; and all others who shared their memories, photographs, stories and expertise regarding Bill Strother as the "Human Spider" or the "Real Santa" of Miller & Rhoads. Along with such assistance, the enthusiasm and encouragement to me from folks to adequately and accurately tell this man's remarkable story is greatly appreciated. Extra loving thanks to my patient, helpful and supportive husband, Bill Deekens.

Any errors are the sole responsibility of the author and not those who offered their assistance.

Introduction

"I BELIEVE!"

"I believe, I believe...It's silly, but I believe!"[1]
—Miracle on 34th Street

I recall my very young days growing up as a girl in a small Hampton Roads community known as Cradock in Portsmouth, Virginia, in the early 1950s. It was a wonderful place to spend my formative years. I remember especially the sweet Christmases with our blue spruce tree decked out with the huge multicolored lights and the strands of silver tinsel that had to be hung tediously one by one, according to the instructions of my dad, Mike Strother. Of course, our dear mom, Evelyn Strother, would offer her suggestions for the tree as well, but her seasonal expertise was wrapping holiday packages and making the delicious Christmas goodies we savored. The finished tree symbol that my sister, Judy, and I had proudly helped decorate and that we thought was so lovely because it "glistened" was erected in the corner of our family room in our modest home on Dahlgren Avenue. Our house was not big by today's standards, but it was the kind of house any child would be proud to call home, especially in the 1950s following the tumultuous years of World War II. It was a white, two-storied house with dark green shutters and a white picket fence. There were a few times at Christmas that I recall it snowed, unusual for the eastern section of Virginia, and looking back on those times today, they remind me of the snowy scenes in the classic holiday film *It's a Wonderful Life*. Indeed, for me, it was "a wonderful life!" And Christmastime brought the visit from *the*

Santa Claus—an event that was so special and so anticipated by me and my family.

Christmas for us was the celebration of the birth of our Savior, Jesus Christ, and we knew that the true reason for the season was to honor him. Also, we knew that Santa Claus, sometimes known, too, as St. Nick or Father Christmas, visited good little girls' and boys' homes at this festive time of year, specifically on Christmas Eve. The excitement of his annual arrival created much enthusiasm and exuberance—bordering on frenzy in our household.

With the exception of Christmas Eve, the one merry holiday event that evoked pure glee from me and my sister and, later, our little brother, John, was the visit to Santaland at the downtown Miller & Rhoads department store in Richmond. The capital of the Commonwealth of Virginia, located only one hundred miles or two hours from our Tidewater home, was a destination location for all folks seeking the "Real Santa." Devoted followers in Virginia, if not all along the East Coast and even perhaps other parts of the United States, absolutely knew that this Santa Claus was the embodiment of all that is just, right and good. This Santa, our Santa, held court at the famous department store on 517 East Broad Street in the 1940s and 1950s. He had declared that Miller & Rhoads was his home away from the North Pole during Christmas, and he had endeared everyone to him since he took up residence at the popular retailer in the early 1940s.

This Santa Claus was the real deal. Since he first came down the chimney in Santaland in 1942 and made his grand entrance into Santaland on the seventh floor, he magically connected with his audience of jubilant children, happy adults and anyone who simply wanted to be a recipient of the joy he exuded. Besides his gregarious but mild-mannered disposition, his somewhat stocky build and his smiling eyes, one simple fact made him so convincing and believable—he addressed each child by name. We *knew* he *must* be *the Real Santa*. We, the children, *knew* he was *the* genuine St. Nicholas from our childhood stories. And, better still, *he truly believed* he was Santa Claus.

This man, Bill Strother, was not only the beloved Santa of my childhood, but we were also related. My father always said we were, but I did not know for certain until my sister traced our family lineage and discovered that our family and Bill Strother are from the same direct Jeremiah Strother line.[2]

Indeed, he was *the* Santa Claus in that era for a multitude of children. But there was much more to this man, this almost bigger-than-life individual. Before he donned the red suit and listened to the hearts' desires of giddy

Top: Nostalgic snow scene photo of the Francis M. Strother family home in Cradock, Portsmouth, Virginia, circa 1955. *Ron and Judy Jones Private Collection.*

Left: Miller & Rhoads in downtown Richmond, Virginia, was the flagship store, and the exterior at Fifth and Grace Streets is pictured here circa 1940s. *Photo by William Edwin Booth, courtesy Virginia Historical Society.*

little ones with his warm, infectious smile, he already had lived an amazing, out-of-the-ordinary life.

This William Carey Strother, the man who would be Santa Claus, previously was known as the "Human Spider," and in some instances, the "Human Fly." From about 1914 to 1926, he climbed countless buildings throughout the United States and Canada. His death-defying feats earned him what would be described today as celebrity status. Strother became known as someone with nerves of steel and skill, with the ability to thrill thousands of spectators from North Carolina to California and even into Canada. Most of his early climbs helped fund the World War I "Liberty Loan" and "Victory Loan" drives, as well as charities such as the Salvation Army, the Elks Club and the Red Cross. These organizations benefited from his exciting yet harrowing exhibitions. Usually, a portion of the collected donations was split and shared between the Spider and the designated beneficiary. Bill discovered it was a lucrative, though perilous, way to make a living.

The Human Spider as he looked just before his successful climb of the Hibernia Bank Building in New Orleans, Louisiana, on April 22, 1919. *Photo by John T. Mendes © The Historic New Orleans Collection, Gift of Waldemar S. Nelson, Acc. No. 2003.0182.194.*

Opposite: Francis "Mike" Strother, Evelyn Strother and their four-year-old daughter, Judith Strother (Jones) celebrate Christmas morning in Portsmouth, Virginia, in 1949. *Ron and Judy Jones Private Collection.*

Bill Strother walks to a window on the seventh floor of the Hibernia Bank Building during his climb on April 22, 1919, in New Orleans. *Photo by John T. Mendes © The Historic New Orleans Collection, Gift of Waldemar S. Nelson, Acc. No. 2003.0182.195.*

Looking back on his scaling buildings as a vocation, truly he was amazing—another Houdini of his time. As the *Jackson County Journal* of Sylva, North Carolina, wrote on May 17, 1918, announcing an upcoming climbing appearance: "THE HUMAN SPIDER, W.C. Strother, will be here and he will climb the Court House and will do many fancy stunts while on top. He will climb without the use of a ladder, rope or anything of the kind, just his hands and feet. HE IS ONE OF THE WORLD'S WONDERS!"

His fame and remarkable skill got the attention of comedian/actor Harold Lloyd in 1922, and Bill became the inspiration for the silent classic film of 1923 *Safety Last!* Lloyd hired Bill to co-star in the movie as the Pal, Limpy Bill (his only cinematic role). He can be seen portraying this character while also doubling as Harold Lloyd's character, the Boy. Dressed as Lloyd, several long shots of Bill were filmed, focusing on his climbing stunts.

Nevertheless, "nothing remains constant," as the saying goes, and circumstances constitute change. My dear paternal grandmother, Ethel

Allen Strother, always said, "Life is a series of adjustments," and changes were in store for Bill Strother. No doubt his age and a bit more body weight made him rethink his career choice. He had experienced a few major falls, and he had commented that the accidents had blunted his focus somewhat; he was not as sharp as he felt he should be. One major fall following some exhibitions promoting *Safety Last!* left him with a serious injury, and he landed in a hospital near Los Angeles. His nurse, Ethel "Grady" Weems, originally from Tennessee, became his wife soon after his hospital stay. She encouraged him to change course. He became a salesman for dog food, but it became obvious he longed for something else.

Mr. and Mrs. Bill Strother decided to purchase a Queen Anne Victorian house in Petersburg, Virginia, in the late 1930s. The city that was a major battleground near the end of the War Between the States would present a new beginning for the couple. They purchased the property and opened it as the Strother House, a boardinghouse or "tourist home." Bill became the designated cook, and both he and his wife enjoyed greeting guests, especially military personnel from the nearby Camp Lee during World War II.

But it seemed that Mrs. Strother sensed that something was missing for her charismatic husband. In 1942, she spotted a notice in the *Richmond Times-Dispatch* that the downtown Richmond flagship department store, Miller & Rhoads, was searching for a Santa Claus. She encouraged Bill to answer the advertisement. He did so and was hired by the enthusiastic store executives, who no doubt recognized his talents and attributes as a performer. In addition, they obviously identified him, too, as someone who loved children (he and Grady did not have any of their own).

Thanks to Strother's theatrical prowess, he and Miller & Rhoads made certain the Santa Claus that would be presented to customers, and indeed to the public in general, would be genuine. His makeup was by Hollywood's Max Factor Jr., and his Christmas red suit was made from the finest velvet with fur from Lyon, France. His boots and belt were Italian leather—no rubber boots for this St. Nick! Everyone agreed he was beautiful and the most genuine-looking and believable Santa in existence! Indeed, he *was* the Real Santa!

He still is *the* Santa to me, and yes, I still believe! As a young child in the 1950s, little did I know that I would later be employed as a Snow Queen at Miller & Rhoads. I worked as a major helper to the famous Santa from 1971 to 1989 (albeit Santa Bill's replacement, Santa Arthur "Chuck" Hood, who carried on "magically" in his own right, with the tradition), until Miller & Rhoads closed and then briefly at Thalhimers until 1991. (Santa Hansford

Sisters Judith Strother (Jones) (left) and Donna Strother (Deekens) visit with the Real Santa, Bill Strother, at Miller & Rhoads in downtown Richmond, Virginia, in 1956. *Bill and Donna Strother Deekens Private Collection.*

Rowe also occupied the chair in Santaland on a part-time basis from 1958 until the mid-1960s. His brother, Santa Dan Rowe, carried on the tradition from the 1960s on, as did Santa Charlie Nuckols and Santa Cullen Johnson in the 1980s until the store's closing.)

The Santa Claus that Bill Strother created, embraced and, yes, *became* set the precedent for the tradition that was honored and offered to customers for the remainder of the store's existence. And that tradition rippled throughout the country into the minds and hearts of those who persevered—and many still strive to do—to spread the spirit of giving year-round, just as Santa Bill had envisioned and hoped others would emulate. The essence of Bill Strother and the Real Santa lives on in the joy and dedication of those who continue in his footsteps. In today's technologically advanced world, where amazement seems to be commonplace, visits to see Santa that produce excitement in children, as well as in the adults who seek to remain young at heart, continue to rank high on the annual Christmas holiday list. The traditional icon of Santa Claus continues to be enhanced by the love and devotion of those who choose to wear the red suit—no doubt, in many cases reverently, in tribute to Bill Strother—echoing a mantra in the Santa Claus international community that is a credit to his legacy: "God bless you and remember to keep the twinkle in your eyes and the spirit of Christmas in your heart."[3]

PART I

SETTING "HIGH" STANDARDS

Chapter 1

YOUNG CAREY

B ill Strother's beginning seemed quite normal for the times. With a background of circumstances representative of the lean economics of many of the communities in the South at the turn of the century, the years ahead for him revealed an exceptional inner spirit, individualism and pride, with an unbridled resourcefulness and a great deal of luck thrown in.

On September 1, 1896, William Carey Strother was born to Simon and Alice Eason Strother in Eureka Town, Nahunta Township, Wayne County, North Carolina.[4] At a young age, Carey, as he was called during his boyhood years, moved with his family to Wilson County to the tobacco-farming community of Stantonsburg, approximately ten miles south of the city of Wilson. According to the 1910 federal census, Simon Strother was employed at a mercantile store, and Alice Strother was a milliner (hat maker) and probably worked in the same store. Simon also served as the postmaster of Stantonsburg.

"Simon was reputed to be a Republican and was famous for only hiring Republicans," laughed Dan Whitley, a ninety-three-year-old native of Stantonsburg, now a retired tobacco and cotton farmer. "Carey was before my time, but I knew his nephew, Paul Jr., who was the son of Carey's brother, Paul Sr.," he said. "We had heard stories of Carey climbing buildings, and we learned local tales telling about when he would come home for a visit."

Whitley continued by saying that young Carey Strother made it known he did not want to be a farmer. "His brother, Paul Sr., was a farmer and also served the community as a rural mail carrier. Paul was a cook in the army in World War I," he added. "There was another brother called 'Bear' [real

Above: The Strother House, homeplace of Bill Strother, still stands in Stantonsburg, North Carolina. Established in 1909, it is owned and operated by the First Baptist Church. *Photo by Donna Strother Deekens. Bill and Donna Strother Deekens Private Collection.*

Left: The Strother House plaque in the front yard of the Strother House in Stantonsburg, North Carolina. The plaque marks the house where William Carey Strother spent his formative years. *Photo by Donna Strother Deekens. Bill and Donna Strother Deekens Private Collection.*

name Staton] who got his name because he was scared after seeing a bear go up a tree in the woods. He ran home and hid under his bed. After that, he was known as 'Bear' from then on," he chuckled.[5]

There were three sisters as well in the family—Eva, Flossie and Mary Macon—according to Carey's great-nephew Nelson Strother, who was born in 1956 and wrote that unfortunately, he never had the pleasure of meeting "Uncle Carey."[6]

The Strother family homeplace can still be seen today in Stantonsburg. It serves as the offices for the First Baptist Church of Stantonsburg, and having had the pleasure of a recent tour kindly conducted by church member Roger Bynum, I was informed that little has changed regarding the layout of the house. "There have been some improvements over the years, but the church did not purchase the house until 1997, from the Page family, who had bought it from the Strothers—Paul Sr. and his children, Paul Jr. and his sister, Jean, who had lived there until 1985," Bynum said. He mentioned that the history of the house can be traced back to Simon and Alice Strother who "set up house keeping" there, according to the commemorative sign posted next to the front-door entrance. A swinging sign on the front lawn is another historic marker that reads "Strother House, Founded, 1909." Mr. and Mrs. Simon Strother, along with their children, were charter members of the Stantonsburg Baptist Church (as it was known at that time). As founding members, Simon and Alice are honored with their framed portraits presented in the foyer of the house, along with other early members of the congregation who helped launch the Baptist tradition in the town.[7]

Such a visit to the home where William Carey Strother spent his childhood was so meaningful to me, as someone who is honored to be the author of his biography. As I walked from room to room, I thought I almost heard the faint voices of the six children who originally were raised there. I envisioned young Carey precipitously climbing up the steep wooden steps, hanging on to the balusters, from the first floor to the second, making his way and precariously sliding down the banister—perhaps as a prelude to what was to come in his career.

Following the informative house tour, Dan and his lovely wife, Marguerite Whitley, and I bid farewell to Roger and expressed our gratitude for his taking the time to open up the house with his master key. What a wonderful opportunity it was to step back in time and experience a sense of the Strother household and young Carey's home life of 1909, with perhaps a glimpse of his boyhood imaginings and aspirations for the future.

Folks in Stantonsburg apparently already knew that little Carey liked to climb, as many young boys do. According to a May 12, 2014 blog posting by the North Carolina Room of the Forsyth County Public Library, as a boy, he had a reputation for being a good tree climber.

In a July 22, 1982 letter to Dr. H.G. Jones of the North Carolina Collection, University of North Carolina Library, Chapel Hill, William Carey Strother's niece Jean D. Strother wrote, "My uncle was fond of climbing, as many boys do, and often climbed buildings in spite of his family trying to get him down."

The bound edition of the *Town of Stantonsburg History*, revised by the historical society in 2004, notes that young Carey was observed climbing the old brick Stantonsburg school (that has been demolished). Many of the residents of Stantonsburg later witnessed him climbing the Cherry Hotel in nearby Wilson. The building still stands at the corner of East Nash and Logan Streets and is known today as the Cherry Apartments.[8]

Carey continued honing his climbing skills on barns, trees and other buildings, especially abandoned ones. Obviously, heights did not bother him, and he scaled edifices as a hobby while walking to and from school. After completing high school, he worked for a short time as a store clerk. Then he decided to go into the real estate business, according to Pulitzer Prize–winning author Clifford Dowdey, who wrote an article on Strother in the December 22, 1951 issue of the *Saturday Evening Post*. In about 1914, Dowdey reported that Bill was working on auction sales for a realty company. "While doing advance promotion on a sale at Kinston, North Carolina, he encountered such apathy that he felt the need of a start to attract a crowd," reported Dowdey. Carey was used to attracting crowds with his climbing, and according to Dowdey, "He did not admit that the human fly was the seventeen-year old auctioneer, but billed himself as 'The Mystery Man,' climbing the four-storied building in Kinston, to an estimated crowd of 5,000 people." The promotional stunt was considered "sensational" and, according to various reports, brought in approximately $35,000 (about $900,000 valued in 2014) in real estate. Dowdey noted that William Carey Strother repeated his promotional daredevil feats in other North Carolina towns where auctions were held.[9]

An article in the *Literary Digest* of April 20, 1918, also heralded W.C. Strother as "the young man who recently startled Atlanta by shinning up the face of the Third National Bank Building." The article quoted a writer from the *Atlanta Journal*, who wrote about Strother, his exploits and his ambitions and referenced his first Kinston climb:

> *He fell, or rather rose, into the spider business quite by accident. He had always been a climber. When the boys went "possum-hunting," they called for Bill to go up the tree. He had a monkey's agility. Used to paint a lot, too. Houses and barns around the country. Never needed a ladder. He'd just shin up a post and swarm all over the roof.*
>
> *Even then Bill had a crowd. His painting was a circus. Give him a roof with a nice slope to it and he would dump a big puddle of paint near the top. Then, a jump into the air, and flop! Bill would land on his bottom-side and slide*

Bill Strother, the Human Spider, climbed the former Cherry Hotel, now the Cherry Apartments, at East Nash and Logan Streets in Wilson, North Carolina, probably around 1918. *Photo by Donna Strother Deekens. Bill and Donna Strother Deekens Private Collection.*

down the roof to the water-spout [sic], *where he hung by his heels. Result—fine long strip of roof painted in half a second. A few more puddles and a few more slides, and he was done. Tough on trousers, but a treat for the folk.*

Three years ago Bill saw a steeple-jack [sic] *climb the county-courthouse. It set him to thinking. He just naturally had a hunch that he could go and*

BILL STROTHER

THE HUMAN SPIDER

CLIMBING FOR

HOME ADDRESS
STANTONSBURG, N. C.

The back side of a calling card for Bill Strother, the Human Spider, which includes not only his name and occupation but also lists his home address as "Stantonsburg, North Carolina," circa 1920. *Bill and Donna Strother Deekens Private Collection.*

Opposite: The front side of a calling card for Bill Strother, the Human Spider, with a promotional climb photo (location unknown), circa 1920. *Bill and Donna Strother Deekens Private Collection.*

do likewise. Still, all he did was think. The bright idea, you see, was only germinating. It continued to germinate while Bill was selling lots for a real-estate company.

One day he was getting ready for an auction sale in Kinston, North Carolina. He had ordered a lot of advertising circulars for the sale, but the train was late.

"Dog gone it!" said Bill to a chap at the corner drugstore. "If those circulars don't come, don't know what I'll do!"

He looked out the window at the court house [sic].

"Reckon I'll have to climb the court house and advertise the sale," he remarked.

The chap in the drugstore was the editor of the daily Kinstonian. *He was hard up for a story that night, so he took a chance.*

The next morning Bill picked up the paper and discovered that he was scheduled to climb the courthouse at 2:00 p.m. Did he back out? He did not. He climbed her from bottom to top in the presence of five thousand people and he sold $35,000 worth of lots.

Bill's bright idea had hit him fair and square by that time. Up until last Christmas he kept on climbing for the real estate company, advertising auction sales, and finally landing in Petersburg, Virginia. There he decided to strike out for himself. He climbed and took up a collection. It netted him $125.

And it was right there that Bill Strother became a spider.[10]

Chapter 2

HANGING OUT

"BUILDERING"

The term "buildering" is not commonly heard these days. Even if one searches the World Wide Web and Googles that word, it asks if the word has been spelled correctly. "Did you mean 'building'?" it asks? No, it's correct: B-U-I-L-D-E-R-I-N-G.

The dictionary (web and print versions) gives the word's meaning as "describing the act of climbing on the outside of buildings and other artificial structures."[11]

Two words—"building" and "bouldering"—are combined to create the term "buildering," so the word is called a portmanteau, according to Wikipedia (en.wikipedia.org/wiki/Buildering). Should the practice of buildering be done without the use of ropes or protection far off the ground, buildering may be considered extremely dangerous. Often, it is an exhibition performed outside legal bounds and performed at night. Even in today's world, buildering, now known as "urban climbing," is practiced on skyscrapers. But certainly, its prominence was between 1910 and 1930.

Adventurers have been climbing heights, especially mountains, for centuries. A skilled alpinist, Geoffrey Winthrop Young, began to experiment climbing the roofs of Cambridge University, England, in 1895. Students there had been scaling the academic architectural edifices for years; however, Young was the first climber to record such an event. He continued his documentation by writing and publishing *The Roof Climber's Guide to Climbing Trinity College Buildings in Cambridge, England.* Then, while at Eton College, he wrote another piece on buildering that served as a spoof on mountaineering.

The Pal, Bill Strother (right), and a fellow construction worker (name unknown) on a steel beam overlooking Fifth and Broad Streets, Los Angeles, California, in *Safety Last!*, 1923. Such "steeplejack" scenes, with accompanying acrobatic antics, were common sights, as depicted in this film that Strother co-starred in with Harold Lloyd. *Courtesy Harold Lloyd Entertainment, Inc.*

In America, buildering began to grow in popularity during the building boom across cities in the United States in the early part of the twentieth century. Steeplejacks dancing on church steeples and steelworkers skipping across grandiose beams offered stunts to passing rubberneckers, who marveled not only at the antics that were presented by these performers but also the impressive, massive building structures that were created at this enterprising time.[12]

The turn of the century brought a new hope, enthusiasm and excitement with an almost "anything goes" philosophy that was not apparent in the late 1800s. Up to that point in time, picnics, parlor games, table games and spectator sports were the entertainment of the day. Prior to prohibition, the early years of the 1900s served as the precursor to usher in the Roaring Twenties era, with sassy speakeasies and the opulence portrayed by such celebrities as novelist F. Scott Fitzgerald and songwriter Cole Porter. About the same time, awe-inspiring sensations were popular, such as magician Harry Houdini, who was a favorite to help sell newspapers with his amazing escapes from restraints.

Climbing daredevils willing to literally test the concrete boundaries with their hands and feet by practicing buildering as a vocation and as entertainment for the masses began making their own headlines. Harry H. Gardner started scaling buildings in 1905. He climbed throughout North America and Europe until about 1923 and successfully reached the top of more than seven hundred structures without special equipment. Another builderer, George Gibson Polley, began climbing buildings in 1910. For Polley's career start, the story goes that the owner of a clothing store promised him a new suit if he scaled the building from the ground floor to the roof, without incident or accident. He made the climb and successfully scampered up as many as two thousand buildings in his career, including the Woolworth Building in New York City in 1920. For that feat, however, he was arrested before he reached the top due to the fact the he failed to obtain an official permit. Both Gardner and Polley, along with other adventurers seeking a type of fame and fortune via a climbing career, billed themselves as the "Human Fly." These two daredevils were fortunate in their climbs. Unfortunately, several other risk-takers who chose such a career path were unlucky in this profession and, sadly, fell to their deaths in their attempts.[13]

On the horizon, another builderer making his mark about the same time was William "Bill" Carey Strother. As early as 1914, he began mesmerizing throngs of spectators who gathered to watch him climb structures as the "Human Spider." He would attempt and successfully ascend one thousand buildings throughout the United States and Canada until about 1926.

For Strother, it was only one facet of an incredible journey.

Chapter 3

"'WILL YOU WALK INTO MY PARLOR?' SAID THE SPIDER TO THE FLY..."

Growing up, perhaps young Carey was familiar with the popular childhood poem "The Spider and the Fly," published in 1829 by English poetess Mary Howitt. Although somewhat sinister and dark, it is also whimsical and amusing. However, there is a diabolical aspect to the moral of the fable: always be leery of what possibly can lurk behind flowery, flattering words delivered eloquently by silver-tongued "spiders" to beautiful but gullible and foolish "flies."

The poem's rhythm is catchy, and the story painted is straightforward to adults but told in an entertaining rhyme that children enjoy, though perhaps not entirely understand. The issues dealt with are trust, safety and death, and ironically, these are issues Bill Strother encountered all through his life, although at different times and in various ways. The poem is worth reviewing:

The Spider and the Fly

"Will you walk into my parlor?" said the spider to the fly;
"Tis the prettiest little parlor that ever you did spy.
The way into my parlor is up a winding stair,
And I have many pretty things to show when you are there."
"O no, no," said the little fly, "To ask me is in vain,
For who goes up your winding stair can ne'er come down again."

"I'm sure you must be weary, dear, with soaring up so high;
Will you rest upon my little bed?" said the spider to the fly.
"There are pretty curtains drawn around, the sheets are fine and thin,
And if you like to rest awhile, I'll snugly tuck you in."
"O no, no," said the little fly, "for I've often heard it said,
They NEVER, NEVER WAKE again, who sleep upon YOUR bed."

Said the cunning spider to the fly, "Dear friend, what shall I do,
To prove the warm affection I've always felt for you?
I have within my pantry good store of all that's nice;
I'm sure you're very welcome; will you please to take a slice?"
"O no, no," said the little fly, "kind sir, that cannot be;
I've heard what's in your pantry, and I do not wish to see."

"Sweet creature!" said the spider, "you're witty and you're wise,
How handsome are your gauzy wings, how brilliant are your eyes!
I have a little looking-glass upon my parlor shelf,
If you'll step in one moment dear, you shall behold yourself."
"I thank you, gentle sir," she said, "for what you're pleased to say,
And bidding you good-morning NOW, I'll call ANOTHER day."

The spider turned him round about, and went into his den,
For well he knew the silly fly would soon be back again:
So he wove a subtle web, in a little corner sly,
And set his table ready to dine upon the fly.
Then he came out to his door again, and merrily did sing,
"Come hither, hither, pretty fly, with the pearl and silver wing:
Your robes are green and purple; there's a crest upon your head;
Your eyes are like the diamond bright, but mine are dull as lead."

Alas, alas! how very soon this silly little fly,
Hearing his wily flattering words, came slowly flitting by.
With buzzing wings she hung aloft, then near and nearer drew,
Thinking only of her crested head—POOR FOOLISH THING! At last,
Up jumped the cunning spider, and fiercely held her fast.
He dragged her up his winding stair, into his dismal den,
Within his little parlor; but she ne'er came out again!

And now, dear little children, who may this story read,
To idle, silly, flattering words, I pray you ne'er give heed;
Unto an evil counselor close heart, and ear, and eye,
And take a lesson from this tale of the Spider and the Fly.[14]

Apparently, those adventurers who climbed buildings in the late 1800s into the early 1900s perceived their craft as that of either the Spider or the Fly, but not in the devilish or naïve descriptions of the insects in the story. No doubt the climbers thought spiders and flies were masterful in their skills, thus their characterizations seemed appropriate. (And of course, later on, *Spiderman* and *The Fly* would become big hit movies as well.)

Newspaper accounts and journal articles beginning around 1918 revealed what seemed to be incredible stories about this "Human Spider" phenomenon, W.C. Strother or Bill Strother, who quickly became a popular local attraction. (He dropped his "Carey" boyhood name for a more professional handle.) Most folks, other than family and Stantonsburg, North Carolina friends, knew him as Bill.[15] And those who knew him did not see him as a conspicuous sort when he was not climbing—except perhaps that he always wore a pink carnation in his lapel.[16]

After he attained his goal in several climbs, this young man perceived that he possessed a unique gift. The idea of getting paid to do what he believed he really was proficient at intrigued him. A trip to Petersburg, Virginia, in January 1918 was another revelation. There, according to the *Wilmington (NC) Morning Star* of February 8, 1918, he witnessed a "Human Fly," George Gibson Polley, of Richmond, Virginia, climb a ten-story building. Admiring what he saw, and with confidence from his Kinston, North Carolina climb a few years before, the twenty-year-old Strother became convinced he could climb buildings, too. So, while in Petersburg, he decided to do more than Polley did and climbed a twelve-story building. Indeed, Bill Strother's tenacity was a positive factor.

About this same time, Bill met another entrepreneurial climber who possessed a similar talent. Harry H. Gardner, another Human Fly, also presented a climbing act, so he and the Human Spider partnered to form their own traveling show. As the Spider and the Fly, they went on the road together, appearing in towns and cities in North Carolina, moving their way south into neighboring South Carolina and then Georgia.

Gardner had been climbing buildings since 1905 and was recognized as a champion of "the risky business." When the two daredevils arrived in Atlanta in February 1918, Harry was the featured attraction, scheduled to climb the

Georgia State Capitol building. He received "star billing." Young Bill, a bit overconfident and anxious to prove himself, challenged the Fly to a "climbing duel." Apparently, Harry Gardner was not amused and refused the proposal.

The Human Spider watched with great interest as the Human Fly made his way upward while dressed in the conventional costume of the time—tights. He completed his ascent in fifty minutes.

Bill noticed that the crowd was still gathered and focused, and he made his way up the building—at first undetected—attired in his street clothes and a derby hat. Attuned to the laughter from the spectators, he worked his audience, throwing in comedy stunts. His performance was enthusiastically received by the spectators, and his climb was completed in twenty minutes, thus whipping his "partner" and wiping out the previous record of the Fly. Gardner was replaced as champion by the ambitious young North Carolinian. Bill soon became recognized as the world champion in this perilous yet potentially profitable profession.[17]

According to the *Literary Digest* of April 20, 1918, after his successful toppling of Gardner from championship status, Strother scaled "everything that would stand without hitching." The *Digest* quoted the *Atlanta Journal* about Bill Strother and his conquests, writing, "He likes to climb, and admits that the thrill is more enticing than the dollars he gets out of it. His climbs have netted him anywhere from $10 on up to $500 a climb. Climbing two or three times a week, he has averaged $100. Pretty good pay, yes, but nobody claims Bill doesn't earn it."[18]

The *Digest* article goes on to report that for his Atlanta climb of the Third National Bank in February 1918, Bill's share was $104. The Human Spider commented, "It was the hardest building I've climbed yet," he said afterward. "Of course, I'm out for the coin, but the real pleasure I get out of it is the crowd. It makes you sweet inside when you look down and the crowd cheers. What is that word? Exult! I exult all over!" he said.[19]

In the interview with Strother, the article added he admitted that the climbing, although it looks pretty easy the way he does it, truly is hard work. He remarked that if folks think it's easy, he is willing to let them try it. "He does not make his efforts the kind that show 'putting on' a lot of style," reported the *Digest*. "He scales the walls of his conquests wearing plain leather shoes and a regular suit and hat. He was criticized by his rivals for donning 'matter-of-fact' clothes, pointing out that he should be wearing rubber shoes and a white suit," the article noted.

Bill said that the most difficult part is holding on with his fingers throughout most of the climb. Indeed, he may be surprised wherever he placed his hand, especially if it's on a slippery spot, and he should lose his grip.

"But," the Spider said, "Once a climber has fallen, he's never as good again. His nerve is gone. He's always a little bit afraid after that."[20]

Nevertheless, Bill noted that anybody with muscle, skill and nerve can climb. According to the *Digest*, he stressed that the single thing one must do to climb is to erase from his mind "the fear of distance." According to Strother, a climber must make himself feel just as much at home on the ledge of the fifteenth story as he does on the sidewalk. If one can do that, then even the comedy stunts that are performed while "airborne" are not difficult, according to his philosophy.

Regarding antics of standing on his head, Bill commented in the article that it is as easy to stand on his head on the roof as on the street. "So," he said, "why shouldn't I do it?" Yes, he may fall, he admitted, but he lost his balance before and "toppled over," and he always managed to catch himself with a quick and calculated turn of his hands.

"It's dangerous business, though, and death always climbs with you," he noted. "In three years, I'll have enough money to quit. Then, it's me for the road!"[21]

Although Bill Strother ascertained that climbing could be lucrative, he also felt the need to give back. Early on, he began climbing for charitable efforts that seemed especially dear to his heart, such as the World War I Liberty and Victory Loan drives.

Too young to be inducted into the service during the outbreak of the war, he offered his climbing appearances that benefited the allied efforts.[22] The United States declared war on Germany on April 6, 1917, and became involved in the conflict that began in Europe in 1914. The U.S. commitment "over there" raged on until November 11, 1918.

There are numerous newspaper accounts of the Human Spider scaling buildings throughout his native Tar Heel State in 1918 at the height of the war. Some records show that perhaps a partnership with another climber was in play at that time. For this collaboration, it was with his friend and mentor, George Gibson Polley who, like Harry Gardner, was billed also as the Human Fly. According to the January 16, 1918 article that ran in the *Lexington (NC) Dispatch*, Strother gave an exhibition in that city "the Thursday before, aided by his advance agent [Polley]." The report read:

> *"Human Spider" Climbs Hotel Wall—W.C. Strother, of Wilson, N.C., who denominates himself the "human spider," gave a splendid imitation of that insect last Thursday night, when he scaled the wall*

Vintage postcard of World War I soldiers called "doughboys," circa 1918. Location unknown. *Bill and Donna Strother Deekens Private Collection.*

of the March Hotel, climbed the flagpole and spun around on its top. Strother was to have given his exhibition in the afternoon, but failed to get here from Winston-Salem on time. His advance agent, who claims to have once been a famous wall scaler, attempted to take his place but was afraid to try the trip over the tin trimmings at the edge of the roof. After a great deal of rambling talk he finally admitted his inability to do the trick. Strother, however, found no trouble in going "over the top," on up the flagpole and seated himself on the little knob. Here he proceeded to make a speech, stuck his hands and feet out in the air and spun around. He then came down part of the way head foremost. His trick was clever indeed and was seen by a large crowd. A collection was taken, of which the Elks got a percentage to devote to war relief work. Strother went from here back to Winston-Salem, where on Saturday he was to repeat his stunt of climbing the O'Hanlon Building.

According to the *Lexington (NC) Dispatch* of January 16, 1918, Bill climbed there on January 10. The article mentioned that "Strother went from here back to Winston-Salem, where on Saturday, [January 12] he was to repeat his stunt [of January 9] of climbing the O'Hanlon Building." [It was reported that he also climbed the Tise Building in Winston-Salem that same afternoon.] Saturday's date is January 12, as stated in the 1918 calendar. Thus, accordingly, Bill went back to Winston-Salem for a second time to climb the O'Hanlon Building on January 12, having already climbed it in early January. Also, it was later reported that the Human Spider climbed the O'Hanlon Building again in January 1919, as well as a return climb in January 1921 (a total of four climbs). The two later excursions were accompanied with his appearances afterward at the Broadway Theater to show his films and answer any questions from the audience.

The January 10, 1918 *Winston-Salem (NC) Journal* ran an article titled "Fear of Distance Quite Unknown to the Human Spider." Regarding Bill's climbs, the reporter wrote:

> *One thing that possibly is unknown to the people who witnessed his performance yesterday is that he maps out his journey step by step to the top of the building before he begins. He knows every step he will take before beginning his trip. He says that he can and frequently does climb buildings blindfolded.*
>
> *The buildings selected to be climbed are usually selected by the advance man, usually a climber himself, and this advance man tells the steps to be taken. Frequently, climbers climb buildings without having seen them before, depending on the drawings, and suggestions of the advance men.*
>
> *Yesterday, he held throngs of people fascinated as he made a perilous climb up the O'Hanlon Building, surmounting ice and slippery footholds as if it were play, finally ascending the flag pole and sharing the breeze of "Old Glory" which was raised by fireman Walter B. Jackson just as it "came over the top."*
>
> *Contrary to general opinion, Mr. Strother began his climb promptly at 4:30, although the recent rains followed by extreme cold made the projecting parts of the building covered with ice. Probably the most exciting moment was when he climbed the flag pole [sic] and Fireman Jackson simultaneously exalted the "Flag of the Free."*

In understanding this "tour" of North Carolina, it is interesting to note the many climbing stunts Bill did along the way. It is amazing that he seemed to possess incredible energy and stamina to travel (by both car and train) and "play" towns and cities one right after the other.

One article from the *Charlotte (NC) News* of January 17, 1918, reported that a large crowd gathered to watch an interesting basketball game the evening of January 16 between the Camp Greene "Quints" and the Eighth Massachusetts team of officers. Greene won thirty-two to nineteen on the court of the Charlotte YMCA. The report added, "The First Connecticut swamped at noon and saw W.C. Strother of Wilson and George Gibson Polley of Richmond, climb the outside wall of the Frank Rich Co."

It was recorded that while in Charlotte, Bill also climbed "the lofty Realty Building" before a large crowd of spectators.

The January 18, 1918 edition of the *Concord (NC) Daily Tribune* announced that the climber arrived in Concord from Charlotte the afternoon of January 17 (after his climb with Polley on January 16). There was no mention of Polley in this particular account; however, he did show up in other newspaper articles regarding Strother's future climbs, mentioned as "The Human Spider's advance agent" but not his climbing partner. (Polley continued to climb buildings until 1927, when tragically, at age twenty-nine, he died of a brain tumor.)

Nevertheless, Bill Strother showed up solo in Concord. The newspaper headlines of January 18 announced: "'Human Spider' Climbs Cabarrus Court House—W.C. Strother of Wilson, the Climber, Will Climb Morris Building Saturday." The text of the account read:

> *"The court house was a pretty hard building to climb," stated W.C. Strother, of Wilson, North Carolina, last night after he had finished a climb from the pavement to the top of the court house tower. The "Human Spider," as he is styled, added that several of the places on the way up were hard to get over, but that he felt confident that he could make the climb before he made the announcement.*
>
> *Without any advance notice, Mr. Strother arrived in Concord late yesterday afternoon from Charlotte, where he climbed the lofty Realty Building before a large crowd of spectators. He announced through a megaphone his intention to climb the court house [sic] at 1:30 o'clock. When asked if it would not then be too dark for him to make the climb, he replied, "I could climb just as well blind-folded."*
>
> *According to his announcement, when the hour came, the "Human Spider" was ready for the feat, which was accomplished before a comparatively small crowd, owing to the fact that very few people knew what was going to be done.*
>
> *In order to give an opportunity to the many people here who would like to see their feat, Mr. Strother has consented to make a return date for Concord, and has announced that he will be here on tomorrow, Saturday, afternoon. At that time he will again climb the Court House [sic] from the ground to the top of the tower.*
>
> *At 4 o'clock in the afternoon, the "Human Spider" will give an exhibition that will doubtless be entirely new to everyone here. He will climb the Morris Building blindfolded. When he gets to the top of the building, he will take a bicycle ride along the top of the building. He will then give three acts in chair-balancing on the ledge of the building, three*

Strother climbed the O'Hanlon Building in Winston-Salem, North Carolina, two times in January 1918. He returned for two more climbs in January 1919 and January 1921. *Courtesy North Carolina Room, Forsyth County Public Library, Winston-Salem, North Carolina.*

stories up in the air. This feat he has performed in a number of cities, and photographs of the act on top of the Tise Building in Winston-Salem are on exhibition here.

Besides climbing the sky scraper [sic] *in Charlotte, Mr. Strother has climbed all the loftiest buildings in practically every building in North Carolina, as well as some of them in New York and other cities. The new O'Hanlon Building in Winston-Salem was climbed easily by him, although the walls were in places coated with ice where the rain had frozen. Not being content with getting on top of that building, he climbed to the top of the flag pole* [sic] *that surmounts that building.*

The young man is a Tar Heel, and has just passed his twenty-first birthday. He has been climbing since a mere lad and has gone up buildings which other climbers have given up as impossible. He is making the climb here for the benefit of the Elks War Relief Fund, and he also in his talk advertises War Savings Stamps and Thrift Stamps as a means for the people to help their government win this war. There is no charge whatever made for seeing these feats, but the spectators are asked to contribute something when the hat is passed, to help build more hospitals and to carry on war relief work. Everyone is invited to come see the climber, and the bigger the crowd the better he likes to climb.[23]

There is evidence that the Human Spider at this time continued on a whirlwind tour of his state. In Greenville, North Carolina, on February 8,

1918, the *Greenville News* reported an interesting insight into the personal life of Bill Strother. The piece revealed he was a smoker. It was titled, "Human Spider is a Great Smoker," and began by quoting him: "No man enjoys a smoke more than I do, but I try not to use tobacco to excess." The article continued and noted, "The Human Spider's dare-deviltry in climbing buildings in many states has electrified tens of thousands of people, and his stunts have been witnessed by a great many people in Greenville as well." The newspaper report went on to explain that Strother was having a discussion with the Mantone medical director regarding the effects of tobacco. The medical director (no name given in the article) was quoted, "To my way of thinking tobacco will not hurt the average man. It certainly has not hurt Strother, and few men have better nerves, strength and health than he."

It is not surprising to this author that Bill was a smoker, given the social acceptance of the day of all forms of tobacco. Also, he hailed from Wilson County, where tobacco was a "king crop" of farms throughout the rural region, and cities such as Wilson and Kinston boasted tobacco markets that yielded economic stability.

Newspaper accounts from North Carolina sources regarding Strother's climbs were not found for the remainder of January 1918, but further research discovered climbing accounts in other Tar Heel locations in February of that year. There is a reference in the February 9, 1918 edition of the *Wilmington (NC) Morning Star* that states, "The Human Spider was performing in many of the towns in western North Carolina during the winter months." It was noted that the event was under the sponsorship of the Elks Club, and a percentage of the collections, secured by passing a hat at the event, went to the charity chosen by that organization.

In the same article, the *Morning Star* made the announcement about the Human Spider's forthcoming climbing exhibition in that city:

> *That part of Wilmington's population that takes delight in thrills, which means about all of the 40,000 or so people who live hereabouts, have the promise of a stampede of creepy feelings in the neighborhood of the spinal column tomorrow afternoon at 12:30, at which hour W.C. Strother, a Wilson, N.C. boy, will climb the face of the American Bank and Trust Co. building at Front and Market streets. And if that does not produce the desired number of thrills, the crowd may gather at the corner of Front and Chestnut at 5:30 and see the daredevil ascend the face of the Murchison.*

Popular tobacco advertisements such as this Girard Cigars ad, circa 1920, ran in magazines and newspapers. Girard Cigars were manufactured in Philadelphia, Pennsylvania, from 1871 to 1926. *Bill and Donna Strother Deekens Private Collection.*

The *Morning Star* reported that, for this climb, George Gibson Polley was billed again as "the Spider's advance agent." The reporter wrote that Polley stated that climbing the Trust Building in Wilmington would not present much difficulty for "the youngster, Bill." But, according to Strother's agent,

While in Wilmington, North Carolina, on February 10, 1918, Strother climbed the American Bank & Trust Building, which can still be viewed today. *Photo by Sally O'Quinn Pace. Joseph B. and Sally O'Quinn Pace Private Collection.*

The Human Spider climbed the Murchison Building on February 10, 1918, in Wilmington, North Carolina. The structure still stands today. *Photo by Sally O'Quinn Pace. Joseph B. and Sally O'Quinn Pace Private Collection.*

the Murchison Building would be a different matter, perhaps presenting difficulties for his former student. "The walls are smooth, the first story being almost insurmountable," Polley said. "The time limit set for scaling the walls is thirty minutes. He will start from the pavement at exactly 5:30 Saturday afternoon, time guaranteed, and at the striking of the hour of six, will be on the top of The Murchison Building, or well, it is a ticklish business!" he added.

The newspaper noted that during the Wilmington climbs, a hat would be passed among the crowds that would gather to witness the events. Strother pledged to give a large portion of his earnings to the Red Cross.

Chapter 4

CLIMBING FOR THE WAR
EFFORT...AND BEYOND

The spring of 1918 saw Bill Strother head back to the western mountains of his state. In an article titled "SYLVA, NC—Red Cross Speakings, Parades, The Human Spider and Others" on May 17, the *Jackson County Journal* in Sylva, North Carolina, reported:

> *One of the biggest rallies ever held in Jackson County will be the Red Cross Rally which will be held here Monday. Hon. D. Haden Ramsey, of Ashville, will deliver an address on the Red Cross, what it is, what it is doing, and what it needs. Mr. Ramsey has a wide reputation as an excellent speaker. The Brass Band from Franklin will furnish music; there will also be some patriotic songs by local talent. A grand parade will be one of the features of the day, led by the band, followed by the Boy Scouts, Camp Fire Girls, Red Cross Nurses and many others. Bill Strother, "The Human Spider," will be there also. He will climb to the top of the Statue on top of the Court House, stand on one foot and make an appeal in behalf of the Red Cross. He will ride a bicycle around the cornice of the building within six inches of the edge; he will also stand on his head on top of the wall and do many other stunts. W.C. Strother is a North Carolina boy who has become famous for his climbing in the past few months and has received more press notoriety for his daring work than any other man in the world ever received in the short time he has been before the public. He has climbed in most of the Southern cities during the past six months. He spent the larger part of last month climbing in the interest of the Liberty Loan. The*

parade will form at twelve o'clock. Every girl and woman in the county is wanted to dress as a Red Cross nurse and march in the parade. Everybody is invited to join the parade.

The *Asheville Citizen* posted a review the next day of Bill's climbing exhibition at the courthouse:

He did it! "Wm. C. Strother," who calls himself the Human Spider and whose specialty is clambering up the walls of high buildings by clinging to tiny crevices and breaks in the wall, climbed the Legal building late yesterday afternoon, according to his promise. Not satisfied with having scaled the wall of the building, the young man conducting a more than mild flirtation with some undertaking establishment, rode a bicycle around the cornice on the top of the building, balanced a chair in a precarious position on the edge of the roof, and stood on his head on the edge of the wall. A large crowd saw the Spider perform, and cheered him when he finally went "over the top." The Spider started on schedule time [sic]. He had to work hard for a time, but after traveling back and forth across the grade of the building, he won his way to the top, and a sigh of relief from the many spectators went up. Climbing up a building is a task, but appears to be sport for the Spider. He has a terrific grip and a trick of holding with his feet on the slightest projection or crevice that enables him to successfully flirt with death at any time. That looks impossible to the layman, climbing a building for all of the hair raising audience.

Strother continued his travels in the western part of the state throughout the month of May. On May 30, 1918, the *Carolina Mountaineer* and *Waynesville (NC) Courier* reported that the young man from Wilson had endured a climbing accident. The newspaper read that the Human Spider, just off from a successful recent climb of the Langren Hotel in Asheville, next scaled the Swain County Courthouse in Bryson City. While he attempted to balance a chair on the dome and stand on his head, the chair gave way and he plummeted twenty-five feet. He was lucky that he sustained only slight injuries. For his performance, although it was cut short, Strother raised $800 for the Red Cross.

It is impossible to track down the complete road schedule for the Human Spider at this point in his climbing travels. It was evident that he could draw crowds, as local newspapers often covered the story and sometimes his appearances even made front-page headlines. Unfortunately, some of the newspaper accounts are lost or not obtainable. In my search, I discovered that many vintage photos of his early climbs simply do not exist. Of the images I located in newspaper archives, their reproduction qualities are poor or the images are unattainable.

Old newspaper articles that were unearthed, however, highlight Bill Strother's "buildering" events and are nonetheless fascinating reports of busy times he experienced on the road. It was a way for him to make a living, and also he continued his philanthropic deeds along the way.

Records show that Bill worked his way north in June 1918 from North Carolina to Virginia. Richmond, Virginia, the "Capital of the Old Dominion," located approximately 175 miles from his native Wilson County in North Carolina, welcomed the young adventurer on June 14. He arrived to climb the Richmond Hotel that same evening on behalf of the Thrift Campaign for the Liberty Loan drive of World War I. The *Richmond Times-Dispatch*, of June 14, 1918, reported that the Human Spider would scale the walls of the hotel at 7:00 p.m. that Friday evening. The article noted:

> *Following a short speech from his automobile, Strother will begin the perilous ascent, clad in his ordinary clothes of a soft shirt and flannel trousers. He will use no net. He estimates that the climb to the roof will consume from fifteen to twenty minutes.*
>
> *The young man who will perform this feat out of pure patriotism and entirely without remuneration, is twenty-one years of age, of mediocre height, and tips the scales at 135 pounds. He is of a particularly wiry build, but otherwise resembles but little the professional athlete.*

The article continued to promote the event with the announcement that once Strother reached the top of the roof of the building, he would ride around the wall on a bicycle. Those witnessing the climb, advised the newspaper, should be forewarned that should the Spider appear to slip while he attempts some of his balancing acts, those incidents may be intentional gestures on his part. Also, the *Times-Dispatch* said that the feats scheduled to be performed at the top of the flagpole will depend on the velocity of the wind at that moment, but that "it will take a pretty stiff breeze to prevent the performer from balancing himself on one foot at that dizzy height."

The date of June 14, reported the newspaper, is the day designated that interest on bonds of the first Liberty Loan became due. According to Harry E. Litchford, the director of the Richmond War Services Society, it was

World War I Liberty Loan pin, circa 1918, from Richmond, Virginia campaign and World War I Victory Loan pin, circa 1919. *Photo by Bill Deekens. Bill and Donna Strother Deekens Private Collection.*

Opposite, top: Bill Strother posed in his automobile and advertised his forthcoming climb of the Richmond Hotel on June 14, 1918, in Richmond, Virginia. *Glass plate negative by Walter Washington Foster. Courtesy Virginia Historical Society.*

Opposite, bottom: Bill Strother in the driver's seat of his automobile, prior to his Richmond Hotel climb on June 14, 1918, in Richmond, Virginia. The gentleman standing is unknown. *Glass plate negative by Walter Washington Foster. Courtesy Virginia Historical Society.*

hoped that those "spectators in attendance that have been clipping coupons from their hands take advantage of the opportunity to turn the funds back into the coffers of the government by making their investment in the thrift program." Also, an appeal was issued calling for at least one hundred Boy Scouts to be on hand to administer the sale of the thrift securities among the crowd.

From Virginia, it appeared that the Spider continued his way north, and by July 3, folks in Harrisburg, Pennsylvania prepared for a fabulous event. The report in the *Evening News* advertised his climb of the Penn-Harris Hotel. The article mentioned, for the first time, that S.A. Hart, Bill Strother's manager, was the one who had made arrangements for the exhibition during the Fourth of July celebration. Hart's anticipatory comments added excitement for Bill's appearance.

"Bill has been over the building and finds with hard work, he will be able to climb up the wall, using only the tips of his fingers," he said. He continued by saying that the Human Spider, on arriving at the top of the building, would stand on his head on the edge of the roof, climb to the top of the flagpole and balance himself on one foot. The climb, according to Hart, would begin immediately following the parade.[24]

The July 6 edition of the *Harrisburg Telegraph* was a follow-up report that hundreds of people witnessed Strother's successful scaling of the Penn-Harris. But the headline read "'Human Spiders' Thrive Under Spell of Strother." The story was an interesting account that expressed the fact that Harrisburg youngsters seemed to be imitating Bill Strother and his talents. Young Harrisburgers were seen in the post office yard walking the high rails. When asked what they were doing, they replied, "Training to become 'Human Spiders!'"[25]

As skilled as he had become, the Human Spider on occasion got caught in his own web and suffered a fall. Continuing a sweep of northeast cities, he arrived in Long Branch, New Jersey, in early September 1918, according to the September 4 issue of the *Red Bank (NJ) Register*. He climbed the Takanassee Hotel that Thursday night and experienced an accident, but it was not the result of a lack of skill or confidence. It was reported that a piece of the building's cornice broke under Strother's weight. He fell approximately twenty feet onto a roof. His injuries were not life-threatening, but he badly sprained one ankle and sustained a deep cut on one elbow. The exhibition was presented as a benefit for the Camp Vail Athletic Fund (for soldiers).

The Spider's schedule presented another climbing feat the very next night at the Second National Bank building in Red Bank. Due to his injuries, he secured the assistance of a local, well-known steeplejack, George Adams of Red Bank, to be his substitute.

The *Register* reported that a large crowd gathered at the designated bank building to witness Bill's climb, and Adams began his ascent up the walls instead. The steeplejack made it part way up the Second National building but stopped and announced that he would climb the Salz & Company store and the W.A. French building instead. He successfully reached the top of the store and satisfied the spectators by performing some acrobatic stunts. A collection for the Camp Vail soldiers was initiated while Adams continued his performance. Bill asked his replacement if he would climb for him the next Monday evening in Atlantic City since the Spider continued to walk with crutches.[26]

The September 17, 1918 edition of the *Wilson (NC) Daily Times*—the home territory of the nomadic Bill Strother—presented a corresponding piece about their favorite son. Echoing what the *Western Mountaineer* and *Waynesville Courier* previously noted, the *Times* reported: "Since Mr. Bill

Strother of Stantonsburg, 'The Human Spider,' exhibited in Wilson, he has been all over the country and though [he] has fallen twice, it was not on account of lack of skill in climbing, but defective walls which caused the trouble."

In the same article, it was reported that prior to the New Jersey accident, he experienced a similar fall. While in Bryson City, North Carolina, near Asheville, on May 25, after he ascended the courthouse and reached the top, Bill attempted to execute the chair-balancing act, when the chair broke beneath him. Luckily, he was only slightly bruised. "A spider could not have fallen more lightly from so great a distance, certainly if he had weighed as much as Strother, who is preparing to serve his country with stunts in the next Liberty Loan drive," the reporter wrote.

Liberty Loan Songbook from World War I, circa 1918. *Bill and Donna Strother Deekens Private Collection.*

As the autumn of that same year rolled by, evidence from other northeastern newspapers and periodicals reported on sightings of the Human Spider. By October 1918, Bill made a full recovery from his injuries. In my research of this man's incredible skill and determination, it is apparent he was not easily dismayed or deterred. Indeed, he was one to "get back up on the horse." He was a man with conviction and one who was very focused and extremely driven. Yes, his efforts were self-promoting but at the same time unselfish, especially for the war effort.

The October 1918 issue of *Variety* confirmed his dedication and patriotism with a report of his climb up the side of the Boardwalk Hotel in Atlantic City, New Jersey. The account stated that when he reached the top, Bill stood on his head. While he performed, the agents of the local Liberty Loan Committee circulated through the crowds and pitched their sales.

Regarding Strother's travels and exhibitions, especially as assistance for the war effort, press coverage of his climbs verified that he performed several times in the New York City area in late October 1918. The *New York Sun* of October 25, 1918, ran an article that promoted a Chinese procession and an Italian procession. Scheduled for the next Saturday night at 7:00 p.m., the parades honored Chinese and Italian soldiers from the city who served in "Uncle Sam's Army." A flag-raising ceremony was scheduled to follow. The announcement read that performers from all entertainment fields had offered their services for the two processions. Bill Strother, the Human Spider, was among the entertainers scheduled to participate, along with others announced, including John Cushing, saxophone artist; Paul Kamerer, civil war bugler; Miss Emma Rolfe; the Zanzies; and Harold Stern performing with his Eighth Coast Guard Artillery Band.

It was noted that Chinese artists were making every effort to beautifully decorate Chinatown, with plans to re-create such a festival as it would have been in China. Local merchants and the Chinese American Citizens Alliance pledged their "carte blanche" support, according to the *Sun*. The newspaper promotion also reported that "sightseeing companies"—Schlessinger's Seeing Chinatown and the Greeley Sight Seeing Cars—offered a donation of 10 percent of their profits garnered Saturday night to be designated for the "Smoke Fund."

In the October 26, 1918 issue of the *Brooklyn Daily Eagle*, under "Stage Notes Broadway," another climb in the New York area that benefited the war effort was announced:

> *Crowds will have a treat this afternoon when Bill Strother, "The Human Spider," will not only climb the Marbridge Building (eleven stories high) at the northeast corner of 34th St. and Broadway, but will balance on his head on the cornice, ride a bicycle on the edge of the building and stand on the top of the flag pole on one foot, while the flag is raised, all for the benefit of the Stage Women's War Relief.*

Many written accounts of Bill Strother's climbs that I have discovered in my research often have featured or made mention of his scaling the Woolworth Building in New York City. Later reports—such as an article that appeared in the *Winnipeg (Manitoba) Tribune* on October 21, 1921, prior to Bill's appearance there—state:

Other notable climbs Mr. Strother has made are, the Woolworth building, 57 stories, which he accomplished by relays, in one hour and 15 minutes; the Singer building, New York, 42 stories high; and the McAlphin Hotel, New York, 30 stories high. Today, Mr. Strother is undisputed champion building climber of the world.[27]

Another later newspaper account, on March 30, 1922, published by the *El Paso Herald*, promoted the Human Spider and his climbing exhibition. It was announced that following the scaling event of the Southwestern Building on the forthcoming Friday evening, there was scheduled a personal appearance of Bill Strother as "an extra added attraction" on the weekend vaudeville bill at the local Crawford Theater. The notice added, "Mr. Strother carries with him a reel of films showing him climbing the Woolworth building in New York City, as well as many other noted buildings."

Although the author of this biography cannot verify with an exact date Strother's scaling of the Woolworth Building, several newspaper reports and articles, such as those noted, mentioned the climb, but no date or time was given. Therefore, I must assume that if Bill Strother did indeed climb those fifty-seven stories of the Woolworth, he must have accomplished it, along with his other New York City conquests, in October 1918. It has been confirmed that during that particular time, he spent many days in the "Big Apple" going from one building to the next, and almost literally "painting the town" on rooftops.

The new year of 1919 brought not only new resolutions but also a new perspective on life. The war was over "over there." It had officially ended on November 11, 1918, and the United States resolved to get back to normal once again.

The Human Spider had served his country well. According to the January 9, 1919 story that appeared in the *Winston-Salem Journal*, by way of his spectacular advertising stunts during the war, "The Spider" had sold over $250,000 in Liberty bonds and $50,000 in war savings stamps and collected more than $28,000 for the Red Cross. (The article noted that this does not include his activities on behalf of other war work.)

Strother's contribution to the war effort was impressive. He must have felt a great sense of pride, and although our country had lost many brave soldiers during the conflict, victory brought freedom.

But, no doubt, Bill knew his work was not over. He and others sensed that it was important to reestablish stability for our country. However, stability involved not only regrouping but also a reaffirmation of our principles

The Woolworth Building, completed in New York, New York, in 1913, is depicted in this vintage postcard, circa 1918. It was a famous structure Strother reportedly climbed. *From* New York, The Empire City—Fifty Colored Views, *circa 1917. Lewis Parks Private Collection.*

Opposite: A Broadway Theater newspaper advertisement appeared in the *Winston-Salem (NC) Journal* on January 8, 1919. The ad announced Strother's appearances following his climbing stunts. *Courtesy North Carolina Room, Forsyth County Public Library, Winston-Salem, North Carolina.*

THE BROADWAY

"The House of Big Pictures." Admission 10c and 20c

ONE TIME TODAY ONLY

GLADYS LESLIE

In

"THE BELOVED IMPOSTER"

The newest Vitagraph feature. Full of situations of intense interest.

EXTRA ADDED ATTRACTION

BILL STROTHER

THE HUMAN SPIDER

Will Climb The O'Hanlon Building Today

At 12:30 Sharp

If you will direct your footsteps to the O'Hanlon Building today you will have occasion to witness a real Daredevil stunt. Not only will he climb the walls but the thrills you will receive after he reaches the top—Well wait and see.

Immediately after performing these stunts he will go to the Broadway Theater, where he can be seen in person and in his own pictures. No advance in prices.

AT THE PILOT TODAY

"The Pick of the Pictures"—Admission 10c and 15c

ONE TIME TODAY ONLY

MAY ALLISON

In

'THE TESTING OF MILDRED VANE'

Metro's Latest Success

AT THE ELMONT TO-DAY

"Pep in Every Program"—Admission 5c and 10c

FOR TODAY ONLY

PEARL WHITE

In

"THE HOUSE OF HATE"

And the Screen Telegram

EXTRA SPECIAL

Be sure to witness the free exhibition on the O'Hanlon Building. Bill Strother the Human Spider, champion climber of the world, will do the trick today at 12;30 and will appear at the BROADWAY THEATER today and Thursday in person and in his own pictures. A good show at the same price.

as a nation, as well as a commitment to reorganize our priorities and to pay our debts. Strother recognized that he needed to continue to perform his daredevil stunts in the interest of the Victory Loan drive, which he immediately embraced. (The Victory Loan of 1919 was instituted as a bond issue to assist with paying off costs of World War I.)[28]

Early in January 1919, the Spider took to the road once more, heading south to his native North Carolina. He arrived in Winston-Salem, and on January 8, he climbed the O'Hanlon Building for a second time within a year. (Earlier in 1915, his friend and Human Fly, George Polley, had attempted to climb the same building but failed.)

According to the *Winston-Salem Journal* article published the day after the O'Hanlon climb, the event was billed as a free exhibition. The reporter wrote, "Mr. Strother furnished the best free exhibition in Winston-Salem since his visit here last year." It was "free" in that tickets were not sold. Such performances nearly

Above: Bill Strother just before he climbed the Hibernia Bank Building in New Orleans on April 22, 1919. Here he implores a large gathering to buy Victory Bonds. *Photo by John T. Mendes © The Historic New Orleans Collection, Gift of Waldemar S. Nelson, Acc. No. 2003.0182.193.*

Left: The Human Spider swings himself over the first big cornice of the Hibernia Bank Building on April 22, 1919, in New Orleans. *Photo by John T. Mendes © The Historic New Orleans Collection, Gift of Waldemar S. Nelson, Acc. No. 2003.0182.161.*

always resulted in passing the hat for the performer, and in Bill Strother's "shows," a percentage of the take usually always went to a charity or worthy cause. The reporter also commented about the Spider that "no small part of his success is due to his clever manager, S.A. Hart." [29]

Following the 12:30 p.m. climb that Wednesday, folks were encouraged to attend an "Extra Special Added Attraction" at the nearby Broadway Theater where the Human Spider was scheduled to appear. It was announced that he would address the audience about his climbs and show his own "moving pictures" of his feats. The lecture and films' presentation was scheduled to be repeated on Thursday, the *Journal* noted.

The spring of 1919 ushered in better weather, and Strother ventured even farther south. The *New Orleans Herald* of April 17 announced that the Human Spider would climb "the tallest building in New Orleans, in the interest of the Victory Loans." It was the Hibernia Bank Building, which he eventually climbed twice. Rare photos of his exhibitions performed on the Hibernia Bank Building were captured on glass plate negatives by John T. Mendez, a local New Orleans photographer whose works are among the holdings of the Historic New Orleans Collection.

After his sensational appearances in Louisiana, Bill traveled to Hattiesburg, Mississippi, and prepared for his climb on Friday, April 25. Billing his appearance as "Victory Loan Day," the *Hattiesburg American* of April 24, 1919, promoted the event with the following headline and story:

> *Fighting Tank and Human Spider Will Feature Victory Loan Day*
> *Soldiers of Shelby are cordially invited to take part in the Victory Loan Day celebration to be held in Hattiesburg Friday afternoon at 2:30 o'clock. A full-armored fighting tank, of the kind used during the war, will take a prominent part in the parade, and one hundred overseas men, white and colored, will be the guard of honor.*
>
> *Bill Strother, the human spider, will be in Hattiesburg Friday and will climb to the top of some tall building in the city. When on top, he will perform some of the most hair-raising, death-inviting, breath-taking feats ever pulled off by any "spider" in America.*
>
> *A parade will be held, leaving the southern station at 2:30 o'clock... The human spider will then perform his feats, beginning at four o'clock.*

For the Spider, the months of both May and June continued to be busy and filled with climbing days due to the availability of pleasant weather. However, newspaper accounts from these months proved to be elusive for research.

But in July 1919, a newspaper article reported that Strother had made his way to the nation's midsection, which presented new challenges for the daredevil, as well as a new manager to help with promotion and exhibitions. According to the July 1, 1919 edition of the *Muskogee (OK) Times-Democrat*, the Human Spider was scheduled to ascend the Phoenix building in that city at 8:00 p.m. that evening. The article read that newly hired manager, Arthur Hill, announced, "Strother will furnish as many thrills as he would on a real skyscraper." Hill added that Bill was scheduled to climb the building, circle the top around the edge with a bicycle and perform other stunts as well.

The *Times-Democrat* noted that Strother claimed he defeated all other Human Spiders and Human Flies and is the champion with an undisputed title.

The reporter wrote that Strother was involved in the war effort and had been instrumental in assisting "Uncle Sam" in the sale of Liberty bonds. It seemed that the Victory Loan appeals by this time had subsided. "He now is climbing for himself," added the reporter.

The end of July 1919 found Bill and his manager in Kansas. The *Wichita Daily Eagle* of July 27 reported:

> *"The Spider" had no trouble in scaling the walls of the Beacon Building Saturday night blindfolded, and made the descent in practically the same way. A crowd witnessed the feat and was as thrilled as the one of Friday night. Strother not only climbed blindfolded, but he interspersed his climb with all the fake falls, slips and other stunts he used the night before. At the eighth story he stood on his head. "The Spider" is accompanied on his trips by Arthur Hill of Houston, who secures the dates and helps with the entertainment. Hill is a professional. During the war, Mr. Hill devoted his talents to government.*
>
> *Sunday morning and evening, Mr. Hill will sing at the Central Church of Christ, Second and Market Streets. Before Strother climbed Saturday night, his manager sang two songs which were well received by the crowd.*

The very next day, the *Daily Eagle* reviewed the climbing event and noted that the Human Spider thrilled Wichita, Kansas, as he scaled the Bitting Building. The article reported that the exhibition benefited the Babies Ice Fund, a charity that raised funds to supply ice for babies whose parents could not afford to buy it. (It was reported in the *Milwaukee Journal* of July 19, 1915, that many babies' illnesses were due to improper feeding. Therefore, milk and ice were supplied for better storage conditions via the Babies Ice Fund.)

Strother's affable manager, Hill, was introduced to the spectators, according to the *Eagle*. He and the Spider left for Hutchinson, Kansas, on Sunday evening. There, Bill tackled the Rorabaugh-Wiley building.[30]

After Kansas, Texas beckoned—Waco, to be specific. No documentation could be found that pinpointed the exact date for the Spider's climb of the Amicable Building there. But a later account, posted on a blog by Randy Fiedler on November 23, 2011, described a trip to Waco for "a return appearance" and mentioned a 1919 exhibition that was staged during the daytime.

Making their way month by month, Strother and Hill continued their cross-country tour, and by October, they had reached the West Coast. On October 11, 1919, in Berkeley, California, the *Berkeley Daily Gazette* announced that an exhibition presented by Bill Strother was scheduled to take place at 7:00 p.m. The notice added, "Hill, ex-soldier, made arrangements with Chief Vollmer for the spectacular climb and the Spider waved all claim to damages in the event of a fall."

Months passed. Newspaper accounts are few and far between of Strother's performances at this particular time, but it is probable they continued. Bill, no doubt, brought "shock and awe" to audiences on a regular basis as he made his way back to the East Coast.

By November 29, 1920, the *Richmond Times-Dispatch* headline stated, "'The Human Fly' to Scale Richmond Hotel Today—Will Also Perform in Airplane During Afternoon If Weather Is Favorable." The announcement read:

> *William Strother, the so-called "Human Spider," will scale the Richmond Hotel this afternoon at 2 o'clock. He uses only his hands in performing the feat. His last ascension* [in Richmond] *was for the benefit of the war-saving stamp campaign, which was then in progress. This time he performs for the benefit of the U.M.C.A. of the Medical College of Virginia.*
>
> *The "Human Spider" arrived in Richmond yesterday in his airplane. After his climbing the Richmond Hotel he will go to either the Fairgrounds or Boulevard Field and perform in his machine. If the weather is not favorable he will postpone his aerial stunts until the following day.*

The reference to Strother's airplane and the announcement that he would do aerial stunts was a surprise to the author and a revelation. To discover a recorded account of this additional extraordinary skill of Bill's was an exciting find!

A follow-up article in the *Times-Dispatch* the next day, November 30, reviewed Strother's appearance and reported that a big crowd turned out

The Richmond Hotel was located at Ninth and Grace Streets across from the Virginia State Capitol, in Richmond, Virginia, circa 1930s. Strother climbed it in 1918 and again in 1920. *Courtesy Valentine Richmond History Center.*

to witness the attempt, made with the aid of only the Spider's bare hands and feet.

The account confirmed that after the climbing event, a huge crowd watched another of Bill's exhibitions. Fortunately, the weather cooperated, and he flew his plane over the city and treated the spectators to a stunning display of aerial stunts.

In early 1921, newspaper accounts reported that the Human Spider continued his climbs while touring the East Coast. He appeared once again at home in North Carolina. The *Greensboro Patriot* of January 31, 1921, ran a piece that described his performance when he scaled the Exchange Bank Building there. The account mentioned that Strother gave the crowd "a fearful fright" when he faked a stunt—"a near tumbler"—after he stood on his head on a windowsill.

In February, Bill remained in the Tar Heel State and made his way to Charlotte. As reported in the *Charlotte News* on February 13, he returned to that city after an absence of two years. The management of the local

Piedmont Theater sponsored the exhibition for the Spider to scale the Realty Building on Monday, February 14, at 7:30 p.m. After his thrilling performance, it was advertised that Strother would be available in person at the Piedmont Theater, in addition to the regular offering of pictures and musical comedy. The reporter wrote, "Mr. Strother is acknowledged as the greatest in his art, and has won that reputation by clear cut work and excelled daring."

The *News* article recalled that the Spider mesmerized Charlotte citizens two years before in a previous climbing appearance of the same building. Following his show of death-defying stunts, the spectators were urged to attend a "thrilling pictorial" at the Piedmont of the Human Spider's most daring exhibitions. The pictorial reviewed his most remarkable climbs and highlighted Strother's new stunt of moving from a speeding automobile to an "aero plane" that traveled up to a speed of ninety miles per hour. It was announced that Bill's upcoming summer schedule included his racing automobiles with "aero planes" at fairs and that he had signed a contract to solidify the deal.

Also, the notice announced that Strother was scheduled to address the audience following the pictorial at the theater. It was anticipated that his comments would explain "how he does it and why he does it, and the sensations he gets while being suspended in midair, trusting only to the grip in his fingers and toes." The climb scheduled for Monday night "will positively be made exactly at 7:30 p.m. by the city clock, and a real exhibition is guaranteed."

Such a declaration from the *Charlotte News* was the first reference discovered by the author regarding Bill Strother's "new stunt" of changing from a speeding automobile to a flying plane by way of a ladder. Later documented archival reports confirmed this initial finding and added another thread of the "wow factor" to the tapestry of this man's remarkable accomplishments.

In March 1921, the Spider headed farther south on a return trip into Georgia. He arrived in Atlanta and on March 31, the announcement was made by the *Atlanta Constitution* that Strother would climb the Citizens and Southern Bank building that evening at 7:30. The exhibition, according to the notice, was sponsored by the American Legion, and proceeds benefited wounded soldiers.

In the article, Bill stated he considered climbing skyscrapers "simple work," with his current main focus executing leaps from a speeding automobile to a flying airplane. He confirmed that such stunts were contracted with fairs for the forthcoming summer of 1921. The *Constitution* reported that the Spider began his climbing career three years earlier in Atlanta (with the Human Fly, Harry Gardner, and their "climbing duel").

A follow-up account the next day, issued by the same newspaper, read that the noted Human Spider postponed his climb from the night before of the Citizen and Southern Bank, due to the threat of pending wet weather.

"Too damp," Bill said. "I'll climb her tomorrow, though, or get caught in my own web trying!"

According to the *Constitution*, Strother "had cast his eyes to the humid heavens late Thursday afternoon, with a foreboding storm that spelled disappointment to the thousands of eager onlookers assembled to watch his dizzy ascent."

The article continued: "'The Spider's' climb will take place on Friday, April 1, at 7:30 p.m. Bill Strother will climb, for he has traveled the unknown way of hundreds of America's skyscrapers throughout the country with the record of still being able to smell the flowers."

Strother climbed his intended conquest Friday night as promised. Reviewing the story in the *Atlanta Constitution* of April 2, 1921, reporter Gladstone Williams wrote a rousing account:

> *"10,000 People See Him Defy All Laws Relating to Gravitation"*
> *Bill Strother, famous human spider, defied the laws of gravity Friday night by blazing a new trail up the Marietta street side of the 14-floor Citizens and Southern Bank building before a crowd estimated at between ten and fifteen thousand spectators. Strother, who hails from the little village of Stantonsburg, N.C., where he got his start climbing on fences, made his appearance at the building on scheduled time exactly at 7:30 o'clock and without wasting much time on ceremonies. He proceeded, five minutes later, to take his life in his own hands as he said by doing something that the thousand and one others considered impossible. "What kind of flowers you want, Bill?" a shrill voice yelled from the seething mob, but the spider had already explained that the benefits from his health-flirtation act were to go to the wounded soldiers' fund, so he yelled back. "Give em to Legion. Give em to the American Legion's wounded soldiers. I don't like flowers. I can't smell!" He then gave his audience the first real thrill of the night. Following his way along the third story [sic] cornice of the building by the aid of a powerful spotlight, he continued up the center section of the wall two stories higher where he nerved himself for the hair-raising feat of standing on his head—both hands and feet dangling free in the air. This he accomplished by raising the window in his path and balancing himself first against the*

half closed aperture, then swinging free of all support, save the reversed portion of his head. This feat was approved by the unrestrained voices of ten thousand onlookers scattered as far down as three blocks way. The climber seemed to enjoy the rumble of applause, for either intentionally or from sheer recklessness, he permitted his body to readjust itself with such a careless twist that it looked as if he was headed for a nose dive into the crowd directly below that scattered. But he was either tooling them or luck was with him, for he came up smiling. Just then someone yelled from a window across the street, "You will never read the story about you in the morning paper[,] Strother!", who by this time was well on his way toward the sixth stop of his journey. Halted in the very middle of the tracks, Strother makes his answer. "We never read the best stories bout any of us, so I'm no worse off than the rest," he shouted back, releasing one hand for megaphone purposes. About two minutes later, he offered the crowd a little more amusement, this time of a different nature, however. It wasn't in the Spider's original schedule to stop at the seventh floor, but upon reaching the window of that division, something changed his mind. The Spider was just fixing to continue his feat by traveling on when either a blonde or brunette "fly"—the spectators couldn't tell from the ground—who perhaps was some pretty steno, attracted Bill's immediate attention by changing the center of gravity to the interior of the office building. Bill pulled the shade down behind him. However, it was the Spider in the fly's parlor, which was a bit against the established rule of things, so for some reason Bill made a quick exit, in which he forgot his hat, and hurriedly continued on his way. Bill didn't stop any more after this until he reached the tenth stanza of his song where the watch was brought into play, showing that ten stories had been scaled in eight minutes. Bill was now within easy hearing distance of his mascot, young Vernon Sues, the young boy who was arrested Thursday night following orders from Washington where it is claimed he ran away from his parents, and who was released Friday morning after a telegram from his mother to the spider authorized the latter to act as guardian for the kid. The kid yelled from the top of the building, "Want a cigarette?" Bill then used the cigarette for a chaser, for some one in the office brought out refreshments. It was a brown, hip pocket size bottle that looked like "Old Times," but Bill turned his back on the crowd for the first time—and the wind was blowing in the wrong direction—so no further evidence was to be had. The glare of the spotlight reflected against the bottle and a stampede was almost started down below. Whatever the contents of the flask were they appeared to offer the necessary stimulation, for Bill made a stop flight from there to the top of the building, where he perfected his feat of dare by posing in a vertical position on the outmost extremity of the roof, with his head the centrifugal point of balance. With this, Bill bid the crowd good night. Officials of the local American Legion, under whose auspices the exhibition was given, expressed themselves as pleased with the collection taken up, and stated that the spider—who already has a record for climbing most of the important buildings of the country—has consented to remain in Atlanta over Monday, when he will add another link to his web by climbing the Winecoff Hotel at 5 o'clock that afternoon.

Like William Tecumseh Sherman during the Civil War, Bill Strother, the Human Spider, had taken Atlanta by storm!

Atlanta requested that Strother stay over until the next Monday, and he agreed to do so to climb the fifteen-story Winecoff Hotel (now the Ellis Hotel). The *Atlanta Constitution* on April 5, 1921, gave the report that his ascension Monday night "was one of the best ever seen in the city due to the fact that he climbed blindfolded." Thousands of onlookers gave him a rousing round of applause.

It was reported, too, by the *Constitution*, that while in Atlanta, Bill Strother filed adoption papers in the court for a twelve-year-old boy, Vernon Sues. The youngster was found by the Spider in High Point, North Carolina, wandering the streets, and Bill began taking him along on his trips. "The kid," as the boy was called, was released into the legal guardianship of Strother. The Spider received permission from the boy's mother, Mrs. Daisy L. Sues, of Denver, Colorado, to keep the child. "The lad has a light tenor voice, and Strother has incorporated the boy's singing talent during the exhibitions," the article noted.[31]

After his appearances in Atlanta, Bill headed southeast and made a stop in Augusta, Georgia. A crowd of approximately five thousand people gathered to watch him maneuver up the seventeen-story Lamar Building. Once on top, the *Augusta Chronicle* reported that the Human Spider performed a headstand on the roof. Strother stayed in the city for a brief time and repeated the climb three days later.[32]

By May 1, 1921, the Human Spider's manager, Art Hill, and "Master" Vernon Sues arrived in Arkansas City, Arkansas. They had come from Wichita, Kansas, where Strother scaled the ten-story Bitting Building for a second time. The next conquest was the Osage Hotel.

According to a feature story written by a reporter for a May 31, 1921 periodical called the *Traveler Info*, the Spider was scheduled to tackle the

This building was once called the Winecoff Hotel in Atlanta, Georgia, when Strother scaled it on April 4, 1921. Today it is known as the Ellis Hotel. *Photo by Bill Deekens. Bill and Donna Strother Deekens Private Collection.*

building on June 1 at 7:30 p.m. The performance would begin with a few songs presented by Art Hill, one being "Buckwheat Cakes," a war song he made popular in army camps while serving as a soldier. Next on the program, "Master Vernon will no doubt give the crowd a treat, offering more tunes with his young golden voice." Also, the story announced, "immediately following the musical numbers, Strother will begin his ascent up the cold bleak side of the hotel building at Summit Street and Central Avenue."

The *Traveler Info* noted that "the trio appeared relaxed and anything but a nervous and anxious lot. While resting in their hotel room, they amicably exchanged stories on topics such as auto racing, etc., rather than focusing on negative subjects such as hair-raising slips between the roof and the ground."

The reporter who interviewed the performers commented to them that the Osage Hotel building presented a nice challenge for Bill.

"Oh, that's a nice little wall to scale," Strother said. "But, what do you think of Milton winning yesterday's race?" According to the reporter, that was the end of the wall-scaling conversation.

The *Traveler Info* piece ended with accolades for Bill Strother and credited him with climbs of the Woolworth Building, the McAlpin Hotel and the Flat Iron Building—all in New York City—as well as numerous others throughout the country.

A review of the Human Spider's performance on June 1, when he scaled the Osage Hotel, appeared in the *Traveler Info* of June 2, 1921:

Human Fly Gives Exhibition
Bill Strother and Party Left City Last Night For Salina
A deathlike calm settled over the crowd as Bill Strother, human spider of repute, started his ascension of the Osage Hotel. Slowly he wended his way upward, while the crowd below gazed in utter astonishment at his steady, careful procedure up the sheer, bleak side of the building.

"Oh, he slipped."

This from a woman fan, for Bill had worked in one of his comedy stunts and let his foot slip from a ledge. He turned, smiled at the crowd, and their anxiety lessened for a minute; but only until he had started up again. At the fifth floor Bill hit a snag. He had no finger hold. Amidst yells from the crowd to come down, save himself, etc. Bill hammered away the resisting mortar and proceeded on to the top of the structure where he, perspiring and breathless, danced about on the narrow ledge, ending with a head stand [sic] on a corner of the building. Then he made an announcement. He was going to scale the walls of the Home National Bank building.

The crowd was peculiarly quiet and meditative as they wended down the street a block. They glanced at the building:

"He'll never do it." "He'll fall." "He can't go over the cornice."

This was heard from every side. With the agility and ease of a man accustomed to such treacherous feats, Bill made it to the third flight, and there he encountered the ledge. The crowd was waiting breathless for his further ascent. Grabbing the cornice stoutly, he swung out over the crowd and kept swinging until with ease he swung once more and "went over the top" and the crowd thought he had completed his venture. Bill stood on his head for a few minutes, then started something else.

With the flag pole [sic] leaning back and forth with his weight, he started his perilous ascent up this point, reached the top, took a seat on top of the gilded ball, and with outstretched arms, he gave a perfect imitation of some ancient statues. The lights playing upon him, dressed all in white, Bill defied all laws of gravitation and common sense while he lingered in this position. He easily slid to the ground, and the evening's entertainment was over.

Many a sigh of relief was heard from the audience as he again appeared on the street.

He and his party left last night for Salina, Kansas, where they will work; and from there, they go to Pueblo and Denver, Colorado.

On June 11, 1921, upon his arrival in Kansas, the *Hutchinson News* posted a notice regarding Strother's newest daredevil attraction:

*Newest and Most Sensational Amusement Ever Attempted—The Human Spider—Will Change From Aero Plane to Car at 75 Miles Per Hour—Tuesday, June 14, Salina, Kansas—Big Auto Races Events—6 * $2,000 in Cash Prizes * 15 Dare Devil Drivers * 50-Mile Free-for-All Auto Races * Come—Come!*

Chapter 5

"O Canada!"

A THRILL RIDE FOR OUR
NEIGHBOR TO THE NORTH

It seems that Bill Strother, the Human Spider, was as much of a major phenomenon in Canada as he was in the United States, if not more so.

There is no documentation available as to why Bill decided to go to Canada to perform his exhibitions.

"He was actually here," said Dr. Donald B. Smith, retired professor emeritus of history at the University of Calgary. "He did climb the two buildings [in Calgary], and it was reported that he talked with a 'Tar Heel' accent. He was extraordinary, this Strother, from what I've seen," he told Michael Futch, a reporter for the *Fayetteville (NC) Observer*, who wrote a story on Bill Strother in 1998.[33]

In early autumn of 1921, Bill and his manager, Arthur R. Hill, amazed Canadians in an impressive three-and-a-half-month sweep of major cities and provinces in Canada, on a whirlwind tour of climbing exhibitions.

According to the September 23, 1921 edition of the *Calgary Herald Daily*, the headlines "heralded" the renowned daredevil and read, "Strothers' Scales the Herald Building, 15,000 Spectators." The article read:

> *In the whole history of Calgary, no such crowd ever gathered within its boundaries as that which assembled in the neighborhood of The Herald Building Thursday evening to witness the most exceptional display of nerve and skill ever seen in this part of Canada, as when Bill Strothers, rightly called the "Human Spider," laughed, joked and climbed his way up every foot of the 12-story Herald building, while more than 15,000 citizens*

Strothers, "The Human Spider" Snapped in Action

Bill Strother is pictured in the *Calgary Daily Herald* climbing the Herald Building in Calgary, Canada, on September 23, 1921. *Dr. Donald B. Smith Private Collection.*

looked on breathlessly. The daring and skill displayed by "The Spider" was a revelation in the power and control of the human mind and body to the thousands of spectators.

While the crowd stood tense and motionless, Bill dressed in white trousers, tennis shoes and a grey cap, scaled every possible section of the huge building on his way up, and flirted with death by purposely slipping at intervals and catching himself with his hands on a sloping window-sill or a precarious-looking piece of stone decoration.

The article noted that the streets of Calgary were packed with people for blocks—"a solid bulk of humanity lined every foot of the sidewalk and pavement during the performance," with roars of applause for the Spider, as he successfully made his way over difficult decorated pieces of the building that protruded eerily from locations on the edifice. (It was later reported that the "monster crowd" was closer to twenty thousand.)

As he made his way up the Herald Building, Strother encountered, between each pair of windows, a semicircular column that appeared marble in nature that ran the height of the structure. The Spider would climb a story or even two at various intervals, only using the inner strength of his hands and knees, as this marble "pole" presented no option of him obtaining a handhold or even a hold from one finger. This stunt was executed by the daredevil at the eighth floor, with absolutely nothing "structure-wise" for him to catch hold of should he slip. Spectators could not believe their eyes.

The *Daily Herald* continued by describing Bill's next trick. After reaching the seventh-story window, he stood on his head, perched on the windowsill and dangled his feet toward the throng below. Only a few moments later, he topped this stunt by doing another headstand on the uppermost cornice of the building. Next, he headed for the center flagpole, conspicuous on the roof and two hundred feet above the ground. Ascending the pole, he situated himself at the top of the large brass ball and nonchalantly read the afternoon edition of the *Calgary Daily Herald*. Following his climb, Bill remarked that the Herald Building was the finest structure he had ever encountered up to that point in his travels of Canada, even though it was the most difficult to scale.

The newspaper article read that the Spider and his pal and manager, Art Hill, were very pleased with the collection taken up for the performance. The funds, to benefit the performer and the local Public Welfare Board, were collected by twenty-five members of the Calgary Elks Club. It was reported that Strother remarked that the Canadians seemed to be more supportive of his efforts and more appreciative of his work than his own native countrymen from the United States.

Further interviews of this amazing man by this documented account revealed additional interesting insights into his psyche, as the account continued.

Strother was asked how he first started climbing buildings, but he replied he really did not know that answer, though he surmised he thought he started out of "mere curiosity." When he went to Kinston, North Carolina, a few miles from his home town, and climbed his first building seven years ago, all the citizens of his town thought he was crazy, and when he returned, they gave him the "cold shoulder," according to the article. The *Daily Herald* continued:

> *This made him very angry, but he had a good opportunity during the war to clear up the score. He went all over the United States during the war, raising money for the* [Liberty] *Victory campaign. He traveled about in a special train, with a full brass band. On one occasion his train was scheduled to pass through his home town, and when the suburbs of the town were reached, he ordered the engines to speed through at 60 miles an hour, and detailed the band to play, "Hail, Hail, the Gang's All Here," on the observation platform, while he went inside the car, pulled down the shades, and gave the hundreds of his fellow townsmen a wide berth as his special whizzed past the station.*

This story that ran in the *Daily Herald* certainly described such an event; however, there is no other documented evidence—in North Carolina or elsewhere—that can validate this information. Strother grew up in Stantonsburg, North Carolina, a town located about dead center between the cities of Wilson and Kinston. No mention of his actual hometown was given in the newspaper piece. One news account, appearing later in the April 14, 1923 *Winnepeg Tribune*, even mentioned that the city of Fayetteville, North Carolina, (over sixty miles away) was Bill's hometown. The *Tribune* reported that Fayetteville was the location where the angry Strother and his traveling company purportedly passed through the depot on a train that was not about to stop for anyone. Looking back, it is probable that this was a folk tale.

But Bill Strother himself was no folk tale. The Palliser Hotel in Calgary presented one more structural challenge for the Spider. He met it with another magnificent show for the approximately fifteen thousand Calgarians who witnessed the climb on September 25, 1921. The *Calgary Daily Herald* headline of September 26 read, "Human Spider Makes Another Startling Climb," but this time, the report included the fact that Bill ascended the ten stories of the hotel—while blindfolded.

A *Herald* representative was at the top on the roof when Strother successfully completed his tricks and waved to the thunderous applause and cheers from the crowd. The reporter mentioned that it was "surprising to note that 'The Spider' was not in the least excited. He might have just completed reading a book and he could not have appeared calmer," the reporter wrote.

The same *Herald* reporter presented to the daredevil that daunting and also haunting question about how he does it as he retired to his dressing room a short time later.

"Oh, I suppose it's will power as much as anything else," Strother answered. "You have to make up your mind you are going to do it! It is the control of the muscles and nerves by the mind, which really makes me become lighter in the air."

The *Herald* article gave a physical and mental description of Bill Strother:

> *He is not a powerfully built man, nor to look at—stripped, a muscular built man, but long sinewy muscles are as hard as steel bands; and especially the muscles stretching from his shoulders across his chest. His hands resemble those of an expert piano player, and are as finely molded as a woman's. They do not convey any signs of unusual strength and in fact, his grasping power is not above that of a normal man of his size.*
>
> *To sum up Bill's success as a climber, depends solely on the fact that he is not afraid to do at a height what he knows he can do on the ground.*

Most people would be too weakened by fear to chin themselves ten stories above a stone pavement, but Bill says he does not experience this sensation. However, he is as dizzy at a height as the normal person, but this dizziness does not seem to smite him with fear.

As with the Herald Building climb, 25 percent of the monies collected from the scaling of the Palliser benefited the local Board of Public Welfare. Again, the exhibition was presented under the auspices of the Calgary Elks. Forty members (instead of the previous twenty-five) circulated among the throng to expedite the collecting of donations and to speed up the performance process. Manager Art Hill had been instrumental in working with organizations such as the Elks, the mayor, the chief of police and commissioner of Calgary, as well as the management for both the Herald Building and the Palliser Hotel. Strother expressed his appreciation to all for the way he had been dealt with and a special thanks for the assistance he received in the technical aspects and arrangements for his climbs.[34]

The Palliser Hotel still stands in 2014, and preparations are under way to celebrate its 100th birthday this summer. Calgary historian Harry Sanders is writing a commemorative book to be published later this year. It is tentatively titled *The Castle by the Tracks: Calgary's Historic Fairmont Palliser Hotel*. Regarding Strother's climb of the Palliser, Sanders wrote,

Fifteen thousand spectators watched as American stuntman Bill Strother— better known as the "Human Spider"—climbed the outside wall of the hotel while blindfolded. According to the Herald, Strother "dangled on the precipice of death during nearly every second of his perilous ascent up the smooth wall and over the impossible looking cornice jutting five feet out from the top of the building. Once at the top, Strother rode a bicycle along the length of the cornice, then climbed the flagpole, lay on his stomach on the round brass ball and kicked out his legs and arms. Then he sat on it and waved a farewell with both hands to the silent, tense thousands below. A sigh of relief swept that throng as he slid to the top of the building, and a roar of applause that fairly shook the building in the neighborhood rent the air.[35]

Another Calgary historian and also an author, Dr. Donald B. Smith is an expert on the era of the 1920s. In 1983, he wrote a book titled *Long Lance: The True Story of an Imposter*. Born Sylvester Clark Long, Long Lance went by the name of "Chief Buffalo Child Long Lance" and attempted to pass himself off as an American Indian. He traveled in a Wild West show and was an advocate for North American Indian rights. Later, he served as a member of the Canadian Army, made appearances as a popular speaker and even earned a reputation to some degree as a writer.

"He was an absolutely fascinating guy," Smith commented about Long Lance in a 1998 article in the *Fayetteville Observer*.

Smith's remarks were in regard to recorded accounts of the meeting of Long Lance and Strother when they appeared together in Calgary in 1921. He confirmed that Long Lance greeted Strother on the roof of the Palliser Hotel on the night of Bill's climb. Somehow they seemed to hit it off pretty well, according to Smith.[36]

In an article on Bill Strother, as told by Long Lance to reporter Bruce Blevins, that ran on the editorial page of the April 14, 1923 *Winnipeg Tribune*, "the Indian" confirmed they shared a room together in Edmonton, Canada, when Bill climbed there. Blevins wrote that according to Long Lance, Strother was twenty-five years old at the time.

Apparently, these particular facts are true. But, as the title of Smith's book declares, Long Lance was an imposter, and most of what he said or wrote has been proven to be tall tales. One such yarn was the story Long Lance described in the *Tribune* of Bill's special train that bypassed his "hometown" of Fayetteville to shun the citizens of the city. Long Lance explained that because of the previous "poor treatment of Strother in the early part of his climbing career, 'the Spider' hated Fayetteville and never returned," and he implied that Bill renounced his native state of North Carolina.[37]

Actually, nothing could be further from the truth. Fayetteville was not Strother's hometown. Chief Buffalo Child Long Lance was wrong, for Bill did not renounce his state.

In 1984, Dr. H.G. Jones of the University of North Carolina in Chapel Hill penned a column that ran in the September 23 edition of the *Durham Sun* (and other AP-syndicated columns). He wrote the article as a retraction for what he presented in the July 22, 1984 edition regarding Strother and his North Carolina roots.

Having read about the revelation that Long Lance was a native North Carolinian and not an American Indian as he portrayed, and that he also was an acquaintance of Strother, Jones was skeptical of the Spider's reputation. He questioned if Bill was a "myth," as Long Lance had proved to be.

It seems that several relatives of Strother read the column in 1984 and took issue with some of the facts. To "set the record straight," Jean D. Strother, Bill's niece, commented in a letter to Jones that she wanted "to correct a few things" regarding how her uncle was portrayed in the column.

"My Uncle was a wonderful man and very proud of the fact that he was a North Carolinian," she wrote.

Jones "was delighted" to receive Jean Strother's letter and ran his retraction that declared, "Bill Strother was no myth."

Reflecting on the Bill Strother–Long Lance association while they were in Canada, Smith wrote:

> *It is quite interesting to note that when the two men met, Bill from North Carolina thought that Sylvester Long Lance was a Cherokee from Oklahoma (which is what he advertised himself as when he came to Calgary). Bill would have no idea that Sylvester actually came from the African American community in Winston-Salem. How different their relationship would be back in their home state!*[58]

After Strother had exited Canada and headed back to the States, the *Calgary Daily Herald* published a letter on November 25, 1921, that was penned from Bill to a Calgary friend. The letter included the most recent information at the time regarding Bill's travels and exploits after Canada. It was mailed two months after his climbing exhibitions there. The *Herald* reported:

> *"The Human Spider's" last conquest was the Wrigley skyscraper in Chicago, which he climbed in zero weather before approximately 50,000 people…Having climbed in Edmonton, Winnipeg, Fort Williams, Toronto, Hamilton and Montreal since leaving Calgary, "the Spider" left Chicago Wednesday for Houston, Texas, to work in the South during the remainder of the winter. The scene of "the Spider's" last Canadian climb was the Windsor Hotel, Montreal.*

Chief Buffalo Child Long Lance committed suicide in 1932.[39]

Chapter 6

CLIMBING TOWARD
AN UNEXPECTED
HOLLYWOOD MOMENT

S trong documentation indicates that Bill Strother made a few interesting stops on his way back from Canada to the United States sometime in late October to mid-November 1921. The letter written to his Calgarian friend that described his recent climb of the Wrigley Building in Chicago in November of that year (the letter not dated but was published in the *Calgary Daily Herald* on November 25) reflected that he was working his way back on United States soil from his successful tour of Canada, eventually ending up in Texas for the winter.

It seems while en route, the Human Spider passed through Bozeman, Montana, and dropped by Aajker Field. There, he paid a visit to Seymour Anderson, who regularly participated in an aerial circus, traveling from community to community throughout the state. An aviator in the Army Air Corps during World War I, Anderson was in the minority of those early military fighter pilots who lived to fly after the war (only 25 percent survived the dangerous training, and the average life expectancy for those in combat was a mere four weeks). He returned home to Montana following the war. These early aviators, called "barnstormers," were daredevils in their own right, originally landing their planes on farms due to the nonexistence of airstrips. Anderson was in the same class as famous aviators of the west in the day such as Charles Lindberg and Wiley Post.

Anderson offered his air shows featuring biplanes, performing aerobatic stunts for the general public that proved popular, particularly in the early 1920s. Although there is not an exact date published of Strother's stop in

Biplanes performing in aerial circuses were popular attractions for all ages following World War I. Here children inspect a landed "aero plane," circa 1920. Location unknown. *Lewis Parks Private Collection.*

Opposite: Another view of the curious children as they admire a biplane following an aerial stunt demonstration, circa 1920. Location unknown. *Lewis Parks Private Collection.*

Bozeman, there is a written account of his performance in Anderson's air circus in 1921.

According to a January 14, 2004 article by Larry Fangler, a staff writer for the *Outlook*, who wrote about "Laurel's Aviation Pioneers," Anderson, in one of his aerial shows, took up Bill Strother. The report noted: "Strothers was standing on his head on a wing of the plane. While Strothers was doing his act, the plane dipped and Anderson was sure Strothers had departed. When Anderson was able to see the wing again, he was pleased to see Strother was still there."

It is not known if there is further documentation that Strother performed more "wingwalking" tricks on biplanes in other air shows, but it is a great probability. And of course, it was discovered that he owned and flew his own plane. This presents yet another thread to the tapestry of Bill Strother's amazing skills and fortitude, and some people might even venture to say "craziness." There is no doubt he possessed a tremendous zest for life, even if the grim reaper was waiting on the sidelines. And somehow, Bill seemed to defy all the odds.

Soon after, Bill and his manager, Art, found themselves in sunny—and warmer—Texas in February 1922. It was a return engagement to Waco for the Spider following a three-year absence.

The Amicable Life Insurance Company Building (ALICO) was his conquest once again, as it had been in 1919, but this time, he scaled it at night, aided by dramatic searchlights. It was reported that it took Strother only forty-three minutes to climb the twenty-two stories. According to the November 11, 2011 blog "Waco, Strange but True: Human Flies and Other Daredevils," posted by Randy Fiedler, once Bill reached the top, he performed some signature tricks. His stunts included doing headstands on the structure's cornices and windowsills, as well as holding onto the building, only by one hand, dangling from its edge. A portion of the proceeds went to charity.

The *Waco News-Tribune* of February 16, 1922, also announced that the Human Spider was scheduled to ascend the Amicable Building on Friday, February 17. The notice read:

> *HUMAN FLY WILL CLIMB AMICABLE—BILL STROTHER IS BACK: AIDS ELKS*
> *After three years of absence from Waco, Bill Strother, the human spider, is back again to take another dash up the walls of the Amicable Life building Friday night with the aid of strong spotlights.*
>
> *Since leaving Waco, Strother and his manager Arthur Hill have made two trips across the continent including a trip across the Dominion of Canada from Vancouver to St. Johns in their three-months and a half tour of Canada where they made every city of size there. They turned over between eight and ten thousand dollars to charity.*
>
> *Death rumors have been numerous concerning Strother. He was reported to have been killed in Omaha more than a year ago. Instead he has been to the top of the 57-story Woolworth building and has done other daring climbing stunts. One of his features Friday evening will be to climb the entire distance of the Amicable at night with the aid of a strong spotlight. Bill wants to see if the perch on top of the Amicable is as comfortable as it was on his last visit, he says.*
>
> *Just prior to the climb, which is being sponsored by the local Elks lodge of Waco, 35 Elks will pass through the crowd with boxes to take up a collection. 50 percent of the proceeds going to their charity relief fund, the other half to Strother for risking his neck.*
>
> *"I am not a blamed fool as some people seem to think I am," says Strother, "and I am not particularly brave or anything of that sort, as some others seem to think. I simply do what the Lord intended me to do. Climbing is a gift and I have it. When I climb I know what I am about. I know what I can do and I do it. Now the crowd watches me and thinks I am going to fall, likely. If they didn't think it was dangerous they wouldn't watch me. Now which has the most sense, the man who knows his business and attends to it or the man who goes to see the fellow work just because the work is in his estimation dangerous.*

Next on the Texas itinerary was San Antonio and the National Bank of Commerce Building. Scheduled to climb the eight-story structure on Friday, March 10, 1922, the Human Spider's exhibition was halted by the city's Police Commissioner Wright. He refused to allow the performance to take place due to the lack of a written permit being filed and disappointed ten thousand spectators, according to the March 13, 1922 issue of the *San Antonio Evening News*.

The account reported that Art Hill secured written permission from Mayor Black's office to allow the climb to be rescheduled for 6:15 p.m. on Tuesday, March 14. "Manager Hill is satisfied that Commissioner Wright will not attempt to stop tomorrow afternoon's climb," the *Evening News* reporter noted. "If he does he will flash Mayor Black's permit. This he was unable to do last Friday, as he only had the Mayor's verbal permission."

The article confirmed that Mayor Black had issued instruction to Lieutenant Miller, who is in charge of traffic, to be certain that here are an ample number of policemen on duty to control the situation and prevent "unnecessary congestion." It was estimated that the crowd would be double in size from the Friday night cancelled climb.

The exhibition was sponsored by the Elks Club of San Antonio. Donations collected from the huge throng by circulating Elks members were donated to charity. The final appearance of the Spider in San Antonio was presented in a spectacular fashion before a "record-breaking crowd" on March 16, 1922, reported the *San Antonio Evening News* of March 17.

Strother made his way meticulously up the walls of the St. Anthony Hotel Building. After reaching the top, he "electrified" the crowd as he rode his bicycle around the perimeter of the roof. According to the report, at one point, the daredevil maneuvered the front wheel of the bicycle so it was completely clear of the structure's cornice. He put such fear in the spectators that they stood stunned when it appeared he would fall to his death.[40]

Texas appearances also included a stop in El Paso and Fort Worth.

The citizens of El Paso welcomed Bill Strother. He and Art Hill arrived in the city from San Antonio, where they had staged performances for the benefit of charity. Prior to that exhibition, the *El Paso Herald* of March 22, 1922, mentioned that the Spider had been making appearances all over Texas and had exhibited his daredevil stunts in Houston. There he climbed on behalf of the *Houston Chronicle* to benefit the sick who were hospitalized at Ellington flying field.

The March 25, 1922 edition of the *Herald* reviewed the exhibition presented by the Human Spider as "one who lived up to publicity and scurried to the top of the Mills Building at 6:15 p.m. [last evening] while greater El Paso observed from below." The climb's proceeds were split between the Salvation Army and Strother.

According to the article, the great number of spectators who attended the event was such that it was difficult to form an estimate. "The crowd packed Santa Jacinto Plaza, incidentally crushing considerable plant life which just was getting started for spring, and so filled streets near and about the east side of the Mills building that automobile traffic almost stopped entirely on the thoroughfares nearly half an hour before the climb was scheduled to start," reported the *Herald*. "It was estimated by Mr. Hill and the 'Spider' that 20,000 persons were in the crowd."[41]

It was announced by Hill that Strother's climb of the fifteen-story First Mortgage Company Building was scheduled to take place Monday afternoon, according to the newspaper report. Hill noted that the Spider ascertained that the First Mortgage Company Building is one of the most difficult to scale in the country due to a major lack of projections to aid in the ascent. Again, the collection would be divided between Strother and the Salvation Army.[42]

Bill Strother stayed in El Paso over a period of several days in March 1922. As advertised, he climbed the First Mortgage Company Building on March 27, in record time, according to the March 28 edition of the *El Paso Herald*:

> *"The Spider" made progress scaling upward, stretching and reaching, moving from window to window. On several occasions, he slipped downward in a precarious manner, holding on solely with the grip of his fingers, on one hand, to prevent him from falling. When he reached the thirteenth floor, Strother stood on his head on the window sill [sic]. Ascending further to the roof, he climbed the flag pole [sic] at the very top. The Salvation Army was the recipient of the funds collected toward the fund drive which began Tuesday.*

As an interesting side story, the *Herald* ran the following piece in the same edition:

> *Small Dog For Pet. Two young men of the "hard-boiled" type, judging from their clothes and the cigarettes dangling from their lips, leaned against an electric light post on a downtown street corner Tuesday. Another young man, neatly dressed and carrying a camera, passed them. This youth held one end of a dog chain. Ambling along at the other end was a dog about*

six inches long and three inches high. The sight amused the two who were draped about the pole. "Can you beat that?" one inquired contemptuously. "Bet his mama tucks him in bed every night and never lets him go out when it's raining." said the other. The youth with the dog did not hear the comments. Perhaps it was just as well for the "hard-boiled" persons that he did not. He was "Bill" Strother, "the human spider," who has climbed the outer face-of the highest buildings in El Paso, not to mention the Woolworth building. He is nationally known as a man of iron nerve.

The Spider's climbing events of El Paso ended with him scaling the front of the Southwestern Building on the evening of March 31, 1922, according to the *Herald* article of that date. The exhibition was sponsored as a feature of an all-day Salvation Army drive.

Previously, there had been a newspaper article that ran in the *Wichita Daily Eagle* on March 29, 1922, that reported Bill Strother was in Paris, France, hoping to climb the Eiffel Tower. The article noted that Strother said he needed exercise and planned "to persuade the French officials to let him climb the famous tower for the benefit of charity. He says he can do it easily."

By researching archival newspapers, the author discovered that Strother actually was in El Paso, Texas, on March 29, 1922. As of this writing, all indications are that the Human Spider never made it to Paris or anywhere in Europe for a climbing exhibition, although most likely he considered the possibility.[43]

In the summer of 1922, Bill finally made his way to the Golden State of California. In June, he was billed to climb Chandler's Furniture Building on Tuesday night at 7:30, announced the June 27, 1922 issue of the *San Bernadino County Sun*. Also, the notice mentioned that Strother visited Colton, California, where he scaled the Anderson Building.

There is little archival evidence regarding Bill's initial time in California. Documentation is evident that he climbed several Los Angeles buildings, including the Lane Mortgage Company building and the Biltmore Hotel, both in 1923. Regarding the Lane Building, Bill climbed it on July 26, 1923, before a reported crowd of thousands, according to film historian and author of *Silent Visions*, John Bengtson. "Strother told the L.A. Times he had climbed buildings throughout the U.S. and Canada, but the conditions for this climb were the most difficult he had ever faced, as the window ledges slant towards the street. Strother's hands were cut and bleeding following the ordeal," wrote Bengtson.[44]

The most interesting and revealing account was Strother's climb of the Brockman Building that occurred a bit earlier, in 1922, and produced a chance meeting between Bill and silent film comedian and star Harold Lloyd. Author and film historian Annette D'Agostino Lloyd, an expert on Lloyd and that innovative era of daring entertainers and thrill-seekers, recalled the climb in her book, *The Harold Lloyd Encyclopedia*:

> *One summer day in 1922, Bill contracted to climb the twelve-story Brockman Building, located on the corner of Seventh Street and Grand Avenue in downtown Los Angeles. That day found Harold Lloyd in the area (it should be remembered that when not wearing his lensless horn-rimmed glasses, the star was virtually unrecognizable):*
>
> *"First place, I was walking down Seventh Street in Los Angeles," explained Lloyd in a 1959 oral history project for Columbia University, "and I noticed at one of the corners this tremendous crowd that was there. And in making inquiries someone told me that a man was going to scale the side of a building, this was about a ten-story building. And, being curious, I waited around, and the man came out and was introduced and said a few remarks, and then proceeded to start to climb up the side of the building. Well, by the time he had climbed up about two stories, and started on the third one, I began to feel so sorry for him, and I said, 'Oh, he can't possibly make it.' It was a very difficult building; he really climbed up just the window—went from one window to the other—I still don't see how he did it. So, being, on, I don't know, a little chicken I guess they call it, I walked on up a block, pretending that I wasn't going to watch him kill himself. But, my curiosity got the better of me, so when I was about a block away, I went around the corner so that I was out of sight, but I could peek around the corner every so often to see where he'd gone. So I watched him scale this whole building by just occasionally peeking at him.*
>
> *"He finally reached the top. Then he got up there, and he had a bicycle, and he rode the bicycle around the edge of the building. Then he got on the flagpole and he stood on his head. Well, it made such a terrific impression on me, and stirred my emotions up to such a degree, that I said, 'My, if it can possibly do that to an adrenal like me, if I can capture that on screen, well, I think I've got something that's never been done before.' So, back I went, and up to the roof where they were, and made myself known, as introduced to the young man that did the scaling, and gave him a card, and told him to come out to the Hal Roach Studios—that we would like to talk with him, that we may have an idea that would be both beneficial to himself and to us."*[245]

Following the chance meeting, Bill Strother was hired by Harold Lloyd and Hal Roach to appear in the film *Safety Last!* Filming began in 1922. Bill was outfitted in costume as Harold Lloyd (complete with straw skimmer) and climbed the International Bank Building in Los Angeles on September 17. Long shots for the movie were made by four cameramen who executed their skills from four different angles that produced a masterful, thrilling sequence for the viewer under the inventive film direction of Fred Newmeyer and Sam Taylor, respectively. Strother had the benefit of being secured to the building by a piano wire—a "safety net" that he was not afforded normally for his climbs. (The International Bank Building was demolished years later and replaced by the Los Angeles City Hall. Fans of the 1950s television series *Superman* will recognize this same building in the opening shot.)[46]

Film historian John Bengtson, author of *Silent Visions*, wrote about the International Bank Building, climbed by Strother, that was used for one of the location shots in Los Angeles in the movie:

The International Savings and Exchange Bank Building (1907–1954) stood at 116 Temple Street. Lloyd's crew constructed a fake clock on the bank building for stuntman Bill Strother's climb. The Bank of Italy (later Bank of America) acquired the building in 1917, staying there until the city purchased it in 1926, with plans to demolish it for the grounds surrounding the new City Hall (1928). The bank was spared the immediate wrecking ball when, in 1927, the city managers decided it could house all of the city Health Department's scattered offices there on a temporary basis, until a permanent, central home for the department was constructed. The sub-basement bank vaults were used to store records, and city clerks dealt with the public through the former tellers' cages. Although a bond measure funding construction of a new Health Department building eventually passed in 1947, it was not built until 1954. The bank was demolished shortly after the Health Department vacated its 27-year-long "temporary" occupancy. At the time, one Bank of America vice-president who had worked there was glad to see the "horrible eyesore" go. A columnist in 1940 once described it as an archaic, architectural menace, and a breeding space for bad smells. (Nostalgic for the 72-hour, seven-day work week, the same columnist also complained that the county workers would soon be switching to a 40-hour, five-day work schedule!) While there is no accounting for taste, admittedly the stately building's wiring and plumbing were ill-functioning and outdated, and the bank was never outfitted with fire escapes. Nonetheless, one can only imagine its once magnificent high-vaulted marble lobby, and the opulent upper-floor offices occupied by the city's early movers and shakers.[47]

Bill Strother, costumed as Harold Lloyd, climbed the International Bank Building on September 17, 1922, in Los Angeles, California, for long shots in the film *Safety Last! Courtesy Marc Wanamaker-Bison Archives.*

Shortly before the major portion of filming was to begin, Bill fell—from the first floor of a building—and broke his leg doing a trick he referred to as a three-story "cake walk climb." He was cast in the film as "the Pal, Limpy Bill."[48] The plot that Lloyd and his creative team came up with works

Top: Bill Strother, dressed as Harold Lloyd, ascends the International Bank Building in 1922, in a uniquely angled shot for the film *Safety Last!* that was released in 1923. *Courtesy Harold Lloyd Entertainment, Inc.*

Left: Strother, as Lloyd, continues to scale the International Bank Building, as cameras follow his ascent in *Safety Last! Courtesy Harold Lloyd Entertainment, Inc.*

well for the story thread—a professional climber (posed as a construction worker) who was committed to make a climb but who had to be replaced by Harold ("the Boy," in the film). Lloyd's comic genius, paired with Strother's seasoned skills, made for a fascinating, mesmerizing combination, producing a type of entertainment never before seen on film. It is Strother's only known cinematic role.[49]

The fourth of Harold Lloyd's "thrill pictures," *Safety Last!* was released on April Fool's Day in 1923 and is considered by many to be Lloyd's crowning achievement among all his ingenious and entertaining films. As Annette D'Agostino Lloyd noted in her *Encyclopedia*, an April 29, 1923 review that ran in the *New York Times* read, "When people are not rocking in their seats at the Strand they will be holding on to the chair arms to keep them 'down!'"[50]

Left: Bill Strother as the Pal, Limpy Bill, in *Safety Last! Courtesy Harold Lloyd Entertainment, Inc.*

Below: The iconic image of Harold Lloyd hanging from the clock in the silent film *Safety Last! Courtesy Harold Lloyd Entertainment, Inc.*

Indeed, *Safety Last!* was a hit in the early days of cinema, and it remains a treasure today to be enjoyed by all ages. It made such an impression on moviegoers in the 1920s that there were those who fainted while watching the climbing sequences. It was documented that some theaters employed nurses or kept ambulances on call to respond to audience members who

Clockwise from top, left: Bill Strother's character, Limpy Bill, begins his climb of the Dresden Apartments in Los Angeles, California, in *Safety Last! Courtesy Harold Lloyd Entertainment, Inc.*; Limpy Bill, eluding a policeman, is halfway up the Dresden Apartments in this shot from *Safety Last! Courtesy Harold Lloyd Entertainment, Inc.*; Limpy Bill is three-fourths up the Dresden Apartments in *Safety Last! Courtesy Harold Lloyd Entertainment, Inc.*; Limpy Bill is seen climbing the top edge of the Dresden Apartments in *Safety Last! Courtesy Harold Lloyd Entertainment, Inc.*

became overwhelmed by the anxiety and excitement.[51] Such extreme reactions from these early movie fans were brought about by Harold Lloyd's formula. He said, "The recipe for thrill pictures is a laugh, a scream and a laugh. Combine screams of apprehension with stomach laughs of comedy and it is hard to fail."[52]

Production costs for the seventy-two-minute film were $120,963, and it grossed $1,588,545. A measure of its success at the box office can be attributed to good publicity. According to Annette D'Agostino Lloyd, a campaign book was issued to complement the release of *Safety Last!* On page three, exhibitors were offered suggestions for publicity:

Secure the services of a human fly. As an ad for a local department store, have him climb the side of their building. Make sure the "fly" has a police permit and that he signs a paper making himself and no one else responsible in case of accident.[53]

Several real-life "human flies," including Strother, climbed to advertise the film in theaters all over the country. Many daredevils performed their publicity stunts successfully, while others were injured. One adventurer, Harry F. Young, fell nine stories to his death while scaling the Hotel Martinique in New York City on March 5, 1923, as a promotion for *Safety Last!* He had lost his life for payment of fifty dollars, leaving behind a wife (who witnessed the fall) and two young sons. One of his earlier conquests had been a successful climb of the Statue of Liberty in New York.[54]

Bill Strother was *the* Human Spider (a nickname he preferred over Human Fly), and his influence for the making of this classic piece of cinematography (not to mention his amazing climbs caught on film) is undeniable. Annette D'Agostino Lloyd, in her encyclopedia on Harold Lloyd, noted, "Bill Strother was, for all intents and purposes, the singular inspiration for Harold Lloyd's most celebrated film, *Safety Last!*"[55]

The film was added to the Library of Congress National Film Registry in 1994. Also, the American Film Institute (AFI) nominated *Safety Last!* for its 1998 and 2007 lists of "100 Years…100 Movies." The image of star Harold Lloyd hanging from the clock in the movie is a recognized icon worldwide.[56]

Who would have ever imagined that young Carey, Bill Strother, of Stantonsburg, Wilson County, North Carolina, could have climbed so high!

Chapter 7

FALLING IN LOVE...BUT ABLE TO LEAP TALL BUILDINGS NO MORE!

Bill Strother's exploits of attempting other climbs in California are sketchy. After the success of *Safety Last!*, it seems he was still climbing, but about late 1922, he suffered a fall (it was not recorded where) and ended up as a patient in a Los Angeles hospital. It is reported that he lost a kidney in the accident, and while he recuperated, he met Ethel "Grady" Weems, a nurse.[57] It seems that while hospitalized, he experienced another "fall," but this time it was of a romantic nature. Bill fell in love with Nurse Weems, who had relocated to California from her native Tennessee. He asked for her hand in marriage, and she accepted.

A copy of the marriage license from Orange County, State of California, of William Carey Strother and Ethel Grady Weems revealed that they were married on February 3, 1923, in Santa Ana, by a Baptist minister, the Reverend Otto Russell. The license reported that Bill was twenty-six years of age and Grady was twenty-five. His occupation listed him as an actor employed with the Hal Roach Studio, and hers was recorded as a nurse. (This record revealed that in February 1923, Bill was still under contract with the Hal Roach Studio. The film *Safety Last!* was released in April of that year.) The couple's residence was listed as Burbank.[58]

Little information is available about Bill and Grady's married life, but all indications are that they were a devoted pair. There is no record of any children, but they both had a great affinity for children, and Bill especially was devoted to his nieces and nephews.[59]

According to Clifford Dowdey's December 22, 1951 *Saturday Evening Post* article, "The World's Highest Paid Santa Claus," Bill's marriage to Grady (who some references call "Mary" or "Mim") was not reason to put an end to his climbing career. Following his complete recovery, he accepted an engagement. Before he left home, Strother informed his bride that he would call her immediately when the climb was over. However, when he ascended the building, he imagined his wife at home and how she would feel in the event she received a phone call from someone with the news that he had fallen. Bill decided then and there that his climbing days were over.[60]

According to an article titled "Taming the Human Fly Feat of Southern Belle" that ran in the *Eugene (OR) Register-Guard* of February 9, 1936, it was not an easy task for Bill to finally halt what he had been involved in for years as a career:

> *Today Bill is tame! The pretty Mary Weems, Southern Belle, did it! Mrs. Strother takes no credit for taming him, and says that her fried chicken, lettuce salad, and strawberry pie did it. She declares, however, that taming lions would be easy compared to what it took to make Bill stop creeping up to breath-taking heights and frightening people... Now Bill can walk past the tallest building without even looking up! He sells dog food to the nation! Perfectly tame!"*

Strother looked earnestly for a job. He knew he needed to reinvent himself and find a new career, and he knew it presented a challenge. He was barely thirty years of age. In late 1923, he reflected on his jobs prior to his climbing years, saying, "I've tried other things, but couldn't make a go of them."[61]

His efforts of muddled picture-making opportunities brought little satisfaction and proved unsuccessful. On one attempt, Bill was paired with humorist and actor Will Rogers. Together they made a few silent films that promptly flopped before they were even completed. Rogers summed up the aborted effort: "How can we get anywhere with me not talking and you not climbing?"[62]

Strother decided to take a hiatus from the entertainment business—at least as it pertained to his particular talents. Instead, he turned to his magnificent dog Ilack, a huge part wolf, part Alaskan husky that weighed 195 pounds and measured six feet two and a half inches when perched on its hind haunches. It was a beautiful, tawny color, and its four legs and paws resembled those of a lion. With the asset of the dog's high IQ, Bill and his canine partner created an act that appeared in both vaudeville shows and pictures. Ilack was seen in the prologue of *The Gold Rush* and also *Lure of the Yukon*.[63] During the Christmas season, the dog worked in Santa Claus shows in Los Angeles–area department stores.[64]

It seemed that Bill and his furry buddy, along with Mrs. Strother, even took their show on the road. An article in the February 15, 1928 edition of the *El Paso Evening Post* reported that Ilack visited the mechanical department of the *Post* in El Paso, along with his owner, Bill Strother, "formerly known as 'The Human Spider.'" The dog, valued at $25,000, also would appear in exhibitions at the O.M. Palm Seed Company the next Thursday, according to the notice. While in El Paso, it was announced that Strother planned to take Ilack to orphanages and children's homes for the youngsters to visit and play with the dog if they would like to do so. Bill commented that the animal was tame and that it was so big, "it can take two or three small children at one time for rides on its back!"

In the late 1920s, Bill returned to his hometown of Stantonsburg, North Carolina, for a visit and had Ilack in tow.

"Carey had his huge dog with him," said Dan Whitley, who still resides in that community. Whitley's late friend and nephew of Bill "Carey" Strother, Paul Strother Jr. liked to tell stories of "Uncle Carey" when the "former Spider" returned home from California for visits.

"It seems Carey came home, and he and his dog visited his brother, Paul Sr., who was working on my family's tobacco farm," Whitley said. "The dog got excited by something he saw or heard in the bushes and took off running. Carey was so upset and looked all over the property until he found him!"[65]

Whitley also recalled stories from local old-timers from years back that revealed that Carey had a fun sense of humor.

"He loved to play tricks on people," chuckled Whitley. One such "victim" was Bennie Shingleton, a local older man who was hard of hearing. "Bennie wore hearing aids and relied on reading people's lips to communicate," Whitley added.

"The story goes that Carey greeted Bennie on the street and just mouthed gibberish to his old friend," laughed Whitley. "Bennie was completely confused, trying to understand what Carey was saying, which was nothing, because he was pretending to talk. Carey had fooled him and got a kick out of it!"[66]

But Bill's pleasant visits home with his wife and his devoted furry friend ended too soon. After returning to California, his dog died.[67] Additionally, the stock market crash of 1929 brought about another obstacle to overcome for not only Strother but also people of every age. Decidedly, the times ahead challenged everyone to the brink.

It was known as the Great Depression.

Chapter 8

"BUDDY, CAN YOU SPARE A DIME?"

The entire nation fell on hard times. Work was difficult, if not impossible, to acquire, as the economy plummeted. Attendance at bread lines and soup kitchens grew, as hope for many, both young and old, dwindled.

Bill Strother experienced a personal depression after the death of his dog. In addition to his deep, emotional loss, he became seriously ill. He was laid up in a hospital in Seattle, Washington, and was concerned that he was going to die. His doctor suggested he get his affairs in order, so he made his will. He turned to prayer but discovered, in attempting to pray, that he was very bitter.[68]

It was a very low point for Bill, and he questioned, "Why should this happen to me?" But as he challenged his approaching death, he saw his wife crying. In that moment, he forgot about his selfish feelings. His prayers were presented again but without protests, and he prayed only that he might be allowed to live for his wife for as long as she was in need of him. Then, a miracle happened—at least, in his view. Soon, he recuperated and remarked, "I felt very close to God. I felt that I had been spared to help others."[69]

But he knew he needed to make a living for himself and his wife and their life together. With his Christian background, he also knew that "the Lord helps those who help themselves." Bill reevaluated his situation and resolved to bring together his entertainment skills, prowess and talents with what he considered "the call." He remembered with fondness the "road shows" with his beloved Ilack, especially performances during the Christmas holidays in department stores. He recalled that the dog had more often than not stolen the show from the Santa Clauses on duty. Bill surmised, with his newfound commitment and philosophy, that this was more a result of what was lacking in the Santas than the amazement of the dog. He came up with ideas that promoted his new revelations that he hoped would be expressed through the Santa Clauses. He presented these initial ideas to various department stores, but they were not well received, and soon he decided to forget them—at least for the moment.[70]

Bill was tired and disillusioned. He wondered where Providence would lead him next, and he knew he could not lose faith.

Chapter 9

HEADING "BACK EAST"

B ill longed for some happy times again. He and his wife decided to go "back East" and visit his North Carolina roots. His father, Simon, had passed away in 1923, but he had other relatives still residing in Stantonsburg. During his travels, Bill and Grady reminisced about their road trips with their dog and the delightful times of stopping and staying at inns and boardinghouses along their route.[71]

About 1936, through some personal connection not known as of this writing, Bill learned about a Queen Anne Victorian home for sale in Petersburg, Virginia, about 175 miles north of Stantonsburg and 23 miles south of Richmond. He and Grady purchased the beautiful home and called it the Strother House. They set out to operate it as a bed-and-breakfast or a "tourist home," as they were commonly called in those days. During World War II, it was a popular boardinghouse for military personnel.[72]

U.S. Census records of 1940 showed that Bill Strother was the proprietor of a "tourist home" in Petersburg, Virginia, and his wife, Ethel Grady Strother, was the "proprietor's partner." Their previous residence in April 1935 was recorded as San Francisco, California. A house servant, "Reginald Neil," was listed as an employee of the tourist home. Neil's place of birth was reported as New York, and his age was thirty-three.[73]

Since Bill's friendly nature was infectious to welcoming guests, the idea seemed like a wonderful one, especially combined with the fact that he was a natural cook.[74]

The Strother House in Petersburg, Virginia, as depicted on a vintage postcard, circa 1940s. *Tim O'Gorman Private Collection.*

The operation of the Strother House by Mr. and Mrs. Strother proved successful for the next eleven years. It had been the perfect solution to Bill's earlier aimlessness and his concern regarding his unsettling nature and his future in general.

Jocelyn Cobb, of Augusta, Georgia, wrote a letter to the editor of the *Augusta Chronicle* on September 19, 1999, and recalled her stay at the Strother House with the couple in the 1940s. The letter read:

> *They settled in Petersburg, Virginia and opened a gloried boarding house [sic], called "The Strother House," serving military personnel from Camp Lee during World War II. They had no trouble keeping it filled to capacity, with every rank and grade from private to general.*
>
> *My husband and I felt most fortunate to get a room there for the duration of his temporary duty assignment.*
>
> *"The Strother House" had an excellent dining room—breakfast and dinner—and who was the cook? It was the former "Human Spider" and Hollywood stuntman—Bill Strother!*

PART II

"SANTA MAGIC!"

Chapter 10

THE MAN WHO WOULD
BE SANTA CLAUS

B ill and Grady Strother enjoyed their roles as hosts of the Strother House. But, like all thriving establishments, the long hours and perfectly executed efforts that produced successful results proved exhausting.

Mrs. Strother sensed that, for her husband, something was still missing in his life. As fate would have it, in 1942, she noticed an advertisement in the *Richmond Times-Dispatch* that announced a search by the downtown Richmond, Virginia flagship department store, Miller & Rhoads, for a Santa Claus. With excitement, Grady presented the notice to Bill and encouraged him to apply for the position.[75]

He read the ad with interest, but he was not eager to portray Santa at that time. Still, he longed to present his "vision" to those who might listen. He thought perhaps this particular venue might be a perfect avenue for the Christmas ideas that he had been harboring in his mind and heart for the past several years.

Bill drove north from Petersburg to the retailer at East Broad Street in Richmond and met with the store executives. He presented an outline to them of the concepts he had accumulated that would hopefully relay to others his simple yet sincere belief that one must rise above selfishness by thinking of others. It was his profound conviction that this universal message that has resonated throughout the ages could be conveyed most appropriately and effectively to audiences when they were most engaged and receptive, as in the case of children at Christmastime.

The store executives listened intently to Bill's ideas and convictions. They were impressed by his presentation and how it could all be incorporated into Miller & Rhoads' ideas and commitment to its customers and the community. His proposal, however, did not include Bill Strother as Santa, and *he* was what the Miller & Rhoads executives wanted for their plan. After all, the store was considered to be one of the most successful and truly customer-oriented retailers in all of Virginia and the East Coast, if not the United States. It was important to offer a "first-rate" Santa operation to the public.

The M&R executives expressed a sincere interest in Strother's vision but on the condition that *he* be Santa Claus. Somewhat taken back by this unexpected "condition" presented to him and anxious to promote his Santa Claus production, Bill decided he would price his services to play Santa, along with his ideas, out of reach so he would be unaffordable for hire. He presented a figure to the store that approximately came to $1,000 a week for four weeks. To his shock and amazement, Miller & Rhoads informed him that he had the job, along with the incorporation of his methods and his heartfelt vision for Santaland.[76]

It was obvious to Strother that there would be no turning back. He embraced his newfound purpose with enthusiasm and traveled to California, where he searched out and reconnected with some of his Hollywood contacts to assist in the creation of his Santa image.

Bill decided to get in touch with the legendary makeup artist Max Factor Jr. On December 14, 1940, an article ran in the *Detroit News* (that ran nationally through the Associated Press) by its motion picture editor, Harold Heffernan, on Santa's appearance was titled "Hollywood Suggests Uniform Conception." It no doubt made an impression on Bill and influenced his plan. The piece read:

> *The legendary make-up artist Max Factor, Jr. and other Hollywood elite make-up artists came together to make some rules to make all Santa actors as similar as possible. They believed that the illusion of Santa must be kept at all cost. These artists came up with a chart called the Standardized Santa Chart (1940 medium height and weight factors). The make-up experts pointed out that Santa's suit, boots, hat, and belt have been standard for years. Their concern was the make-up, hair length, and size of the man portraying the Jolly Old Elf. Following are the tips that Hollywood will use for years: The characterization should be aged to around 70 years of age. All make-up created should have this in mind. The whiskers, hair, and moustache should be of pure yak hair with a definite wave and curl*

with a minimum drop of 12" and a maximum drop of 16". (That's for the whiskers measured from the lower lip.) If using a natural beard the minimum drop should be 10". The hair should be shoulder length. Santa should have matching busy eyebrows with a little salt and pepper look. Highlight the nose with #14 red rouge. The height should be no shorter than 5'9" and no taller than 6'0". Weight should range from 180 lbs. to 215 lbs. The padded girth would be 48" to 52". The make up wizards pointed out that a Santa body type would be similar to W.C. Fields and Wallace Berry.

Phillip L. Wenz, a charter member of the International Santa Claus Hall of Fame, in Santa Claus, Indiana, agrees that the "Standardized Santa Chart" became an instrumental guide and is still referenced today. "Now remember," Wenz said, "this is 1940, so the measurements were taken from the medium height and weight considerations of the day." [77]

As Bill met with Factor and others in California to create the look, the "Santa Standards" were fine-tuned. By 1947, articles ran throughout the country explaining the importance of the guidelines. An Associated Press feature article that ran out of Hollywood appeared in the December 18, 1947 edition of the *Kokomo (IN) Tribune*:

A veteran Santa Claus and a veteran make-up man today solved the daughter's inquiry question for parents: Why does not Santa at Macy's look like Santa at Gimbels? They set up standards for Santa Claus. Next year, if the experts can sell their formula to the Santa Claus association, you won't have to explain to the kiddies how Kris Kringle on another street corner has lost 30 pounds and grown six inches of whiskers after they saw him two blocks away. The standards were set up by Max Factor Jr., movie make-up authority, and William C. Strother of Richmond, VA., a veteran year-round Santa and instructor of apprentice Santas. "I've had lots of kids ask me how come I'd changed so much since they saw Santa last week." Strother said. "It's disillusioning; kind of gets a kid to wondering." Santa Claus and the make-up man combined their experience and decided that every yuletide saint should be around five feet, nine inches. If he can't make it with elevator shoes, he ought to wear a higher hat. He should be padded out or pounded in to a plump 185 IBS., neither too fat nor too thin. Bushy white eyebrows must seal his real brows and standardize his eyes and forehead, the experts said. The white mustache hides a multitude of mouths. It ought to droop down over the lip and curl up around the nose.

All beards, the experts said, should be 12 inches in length. "The kids can tell the difference," Strother said, "by where it tickles them." They prescribe rouge for the nose, cheeks and ears, and some face powder for pale complexions. An experienced Santa Claus, Strother said he found his clients much more likely to notice that his face was different from other Santas than that his clothes were. "You can always tell the children your other suit is out being pressed because you got caught in a snowstorm," Strother said, "but what will you tell them about your other stomach?"

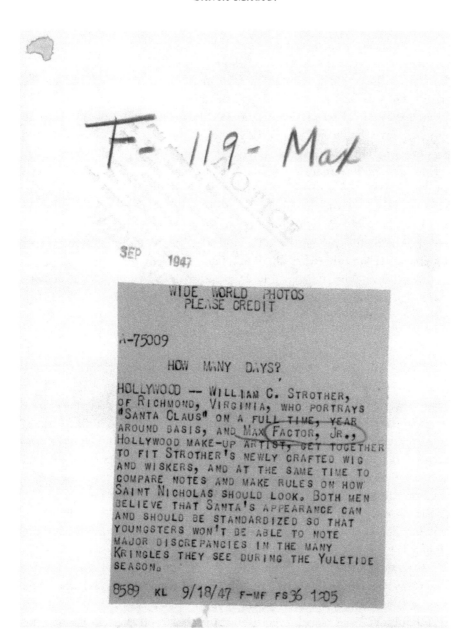

F- 119 - Max

SEP 1947

WIDE WORLD PHOTOS
PLEASE CREDIT

A-75009

HOW MANY DAYS?

HOLLYWOOD — WILLIAM C. STROTHER,
OF RICHMOND, VIRGINIA, WHO PORTRAYS
"SANTA CLAUS" ON A FULL TIME, YEAR
AROUND BASIS, AND MAX FACTOR, JR.,
HOLLYWOOD MAKE-UP ARTIST, GET TOGETHER
TO FIT STROTHER'S NEWLY CRAFTED WIG
AND WISKERS, AND AT THE SAME TIME TO
COMPARE NOTES AND MAKE RULES ON HOW
SAINT NICHOLAS SHOULD LOOK. BOTH MEN
BELIEVE THAT SANTA'S APPEARANCE CAN
AND SHOULD BE STANDARDIZED SO THAT
YOUNGSTERS WON'T BE ABLE TO NOTE
MAJOR DISCREPANCIES IN THE MANY
KRINGLES THEY SEE DURING THE YULETIDE
SEASON.

8589 KL 9/18/47 F-MF FS36 1205

Back side of press photo of makeup artist Max Factor Jr. and Santa Bill Strother. Description information ran with the photo that was distributed to newspapers nationwide. *Courtesy press photo, Wide World Photos, 1947, Historic Images.*

Opposite: Hollywood makeup artist Max Factor Jr. was instrumental in helping to create the Real Santa look for Bill Strother in the 1940s. *Courtesy press photo, Wide World Photos, 1947, Historic Images.*

Bill's makeup was perfected, and the results included a wig, beard, mustache and eyebrows that totaled $500. It was determined that the pieces must be replaced on a regular basis to maintain a freshness and lifelike quality. He was taught to use rouge that did not contain grease paint. He learned that such tricks reflected the red and white colors of his costume and thus gave the illusion of a ruddy complexion produced by exposure to the outdoors.[78]

Strother's endorsement by Miller & Rhoads of becoming *the* Santa was cemented even more with his red suit. Retired store executive George Bryson, who was a part of the downtown store in the 1950s, remarked that at the time of Bill's hiring, Penn Montague, M&R's director of interior display, was in charge of Santa's props. "Penn told me once that Santa Bill's mystique was tangible as well as otherwise," Bryson wrote. "Bill demanded [a] custom wig and beard from Max Factor of Hollywood; real white [rabbit] fur; custom made [leather] boots; and a suit of French Lyon velvet costing $25.00 a yard then. That's about $200.00 a yard in today's dollars. Obviously, he outclassed all the competition in appearance, plus he could remove his cap!" he added.[79]

Bill's creativity and imagination went far beyond merely his elaborate makeup and ideal red suit. He suggested to the store's executives that a track be built around the edge of the roof of the Miller & Rhoads building. There he envisioned that electric reindeer would pull him and transport him around the perimeter in an open sleigh. Once off the sleigh, he would climb up the twenty-foot "fake" chimney and enter it, feet first, from the top. But the grand idea dissipated when the city refused to issue a permit for the stunt.[80]

Chris Rhoads, the son of one of the stores' founders, Webster Rhoads Jr., said his father was not for the idea of Santa climbing the sides of the M&R building. Former store executive George Bryson, who coauthored with Earle Dunford a history of the retailer titled *Under the Clock: The Story of Miller & Rhoads*, said the story was worthy to be included in their book. Webster Rhoads is reported to have said about Bill and his climbing concept, "You may be 'The Human Spider,' but I'm not going to let you kill Santa Claus!"[81]

Although Bill was not allowed to introduce his rooftop tricks, he was not to be easily dismayed. His idea of climbing down a chimney continued to intrigue him, so he decided to incorporate it inside the store in Santaland. He thought it just as convincing "to appear to children as Santa Claus had traditionally appeared in their imaginations."[82]

But coming down the chimney in Santaland (that had been transformed from the Old Dominion Room on the seventh floor), Santa Bill, having become heavier since his "Spider" days, suffered a fall on the first day of his appearance. The mishap occurred as he climbed into a device that lowered him onto the stage for his meeting with children. He injured his shoulder and suffered through incessant pain that especially affected his sleeping. Yet it was in this period of physical pain and anguish that Strother truly transformed himself into Santa Claus.[83]

According to the December 22, 1951 article "The World's Highest Paid Santa Claus," in the *Saturday Evening Post*, writer Clifford Dowdey explained:

> *Though no actor, his original notion, once he took the job, had been to make a good show of it. When he first saw the expectant faces of the children, he was profoundly moved. He said, "They won my heart and I forgot all about acting. I put everything of myself into what I was doing, and each child become as precious to me as if they were my own flesh and blood. In the next days, when the pain in my shoulder was terrible, the only rest I could get was when I was with the children. With them the pain went away."*[84]

Dowdey added that Bill Strother had "reaffirmed the truth of his own lesson of forgetting self, and from then on he could truly be said to lose himself in the part. Not acting as something he isn't, his identification with Santa Claus is complete. 'The children know…,' Strother said."[85]

In those early years, Santa Bill offered two shows at the store. Jingling sleigh bells introduced these morning and afternoon spectaculars, held in the "North Pole" Santaland setting of a winter wonderland of sparkling and twinkling stars. Then the black, shiny leather boots appeared—first one, then the other—dropping down from the center of the fireplace that was located on the platform stage decorated with Santa's throne. Also in view was the Snow Queen's chair and a beautiful shimmering Christmas tree, with brightly wrapped packages and toys beneath its branches.

Next, the Christmas red of Santa's pants came into view. His boots touched the floor with a solid *thud!* Santa Claus emerged as he bent down first to clear the brick fireplace that was part of a mantelpiece, festively decorated with hanging holiday stockings. Complete with a pack on his back, Santa greeted the waiting crowd, "his blue eyes merry beneath frosty eyebrows; and, above his snowy beard, the ruddy glow of his cheeks looked as if he had just finished 'a wintry night's ride in an open sleigh.'"[86]

Santa made his way to his adorned chair and prepared for his visit from the children. Each child made his and her way to him one by one and, en

route, stopped by the chair of the Snow Queen, seated at his right. The Snow Queen, dressed all in white, except for her twinkling, silvery crown, greeted the youngsters with a smile and a calming presence. The little visitors chatted with her briefly and shared their names and sometimes their wishes and dreams for Christmas.

Up to this point, the setting truly was endearing and memorable, and with the anticipation and excitement of the actual visit with Santa, the children were in awe. The mesmerizing moment came when they first met with Santa's helper, the Snow Queen, and what happened next, through an almost ethereal connection, Santa greeted them personally by their names. Of course, the children accepted it as a natural thing—"Santa Claus knew my name!" The audience watching, however, many of them parents of the visiting youngsters, often seemed perplexed and even baffled by what they witnessed. To this day, many folks still accept the fact that he was the Real Santa, and it was simply "Santa magic!"

This "magical" element to his show was the most captivating aspect of this Santa and a visit to Miller & Rhoads during the yuletide season. It was so astonishing that it was patented for the first twenty years. This

Santa Bill and Snow Queen Jean Richardson meet with Scott and Penn Burke at Miller & Rhoads, 1954. *Penn Burke Private Collection.*

Opposite: Santa Bill enters Santaland at the downtown Richmond, Virginia M&R—coming down the chimney—circa 1952. This innovative idea was one aspect of his Real Santa. *Photo by Flournoy. Courtesy Virginia Chamber of Commerce, Valentine Richmond History Center.*

Santa Bill greets his admiring audience from the Santaland stage at Miller & Rhoads in downtown Richmond, circa 1952. *Photo by Flournoy. Courtesy Virginia Chamber of Commerce, Valentine Richmond History Center.*

phenomenal "Santa-child visit" was specifically characteristic of the Real Santa only located at this store in Richmond. This performance art was Santa Bill's way of relaying his message to all children of the gift of the spirit of Christmas and a giving heart. Miller & Rhoads presented him with the chance to offer this enchanting moment in time, and he made it his own.

This Santa made a concentrated effort to genuinely connect with the children who often waited in line for hours for this unique and spellbinding encounter. Once the child reached him, his soft melodious voice did not just open the conversation with "What do you want for Christmas?" Instead, he told them about the true spirit of the holiday season. In a direct appeal to each youngster—in terms only a little one would understand and take to heart—he explained the importance of a belief in the joys of giving and the practice of unselfishness. He stressed the significance of the blessing of service to others, especially to their parents and family. He was gentle, kind and patient in each meeting and greeted the children with an honest interest in them as if each one was the most important person in the world at that moment, which almost put the children in a trance. His manner, warmth and evident dedication to his calling personified his commitment to what he considered the most important thing he could give to them from his heart—the gift of love.[87]

But Santa Bill also inquired about what the youngsters might be wishing for at Christmas. He remarked that he felt their dreams were important, but he emphasized that he tried to play down the "gimme" aspect, as the commercialism of the holidays concerned him. He believed in hopes and aspirations and commented, "The most important thing in the world is that dreams come true. It's as important for grown-ups as for children."[88]

Anyone and everyone who visited Miller & Rhoads' Santaland from 1942 to 1956 was enamored with this most beloved Santa. In a feature article written by Clifford Dowdey for the December 1957 issue of the *Virginia Record*, he expressed that Bill Strother "possessed the potential of making him the most realistic and appealing Santa Claus ever imagined, and Miller & Rhoads gave him the opportunity."[89]

Indeed, more than fifteen thousand children were reported to have visited with him in his early reign, and the numbers climbed through the years.

Especially during the years that World War II raged, Miller & Rhoads continued to help keep the "home fires burning" and operated "business as usual." But everyone knew that business as usual also required the store to be a participant in the war effort, just like everyone else. The store's windows promoted patriotism and prayers, as well as war bonds and scrap metal drives for the cause.[90]

It was important for Santa to still present his smiles and his gracious manner in this fragile time in our history. His convictions of what is good and just and his determination to promote the elements of love and goodwill were especially important for a weary public—both children and adults alike. He viewed his role as Santa as such an important one that his friends said that it was a religion to him.[91]

John Marchant, who served as a president of Miller & Rhoads, remarked, "That wonderful Santa Claus thought he *was* Santa Claus!"[92]

Of course, all the children—and even their parents—could tell you he was the Real Santa as well. Santa Bill once commented in an interview that no child had asked him on any occasion if his whiskers were real. "They take it for granted that my whiskers are real, because to them Santa Claus is real, and Santa Claus has whiskers," he said.[93]

AIR RAID PROTECTION
FOR PEOPLE IN MILLER & RHOADS

Keep calm our Employees are organized to help you.

You will be safer in our store than on the street.

Our doors will remain open so if you are caught on the street we will be glad to have you come in.

SAFETY FLOORS are Second and Third
[Grace Street Side.]

Go there by Escalators, or the Fireproof Stairways on the Grace Street side.

WALK - DO NOT RUN.

Follow instructions given over the loud speaker system and by Store Wardens.

To talk with adults today who were children of the 1940s and '50s, visiting Santa at Miller & Rhoads in downtown Richmond, there was never any doubt that he was the genuine article. Linda Baldwin Scott remembered her visit with this very special Jolly Old Elf in the 1950s, specifically Christmas of 1956.

"Entering Santaland on the seventh floor was enchanting, for in my mind it was a 'magical land,'" recalled Ms. Scott. "He was so welcoming with his soft, calming voice. I was so excited before my visit, and I was told by my family that this was something we would do every year, and this was something that we would remember forever. We did believe he was the Real Santa and we did go back every year!" she added.

"Our parents said we were only allowed to ask for one thing. I remember I asked him for a Tiny Tears doll that year," Mrs. Scott noted.

"I distinctly remember him calling me by my name—that's what made it so special!" she said with a smile. "This Santa provided for me a very personal, comfortable feeling. I had been adopted and I knew that, and visiting with him gave me such a secure feeling. He had an aura about him and evoked love and joy that lives on in my heart today, and I know it will always be there as long as I seek to remember and still believe!"[94]

Dear Santa Claus

I am not asking for much this Christmas because there is a war on. I just want one thing and that is a Machine Gun no. 42-70. I saw it in the F.A.O. Schwarz magzine. I hope you have anought toys for everybody this Christmas.

your friend
Jackie Robertson.

Letter to Santa Claus from Jaquelin T. Robertson, circa 1944. *Courtesy Virginia Historical Society.*

Opposite: Miller & Rhoads, committed to the World War II effort, posted air raid posters throughout the store, circa 1943. *Penn Burke Private Collection.*

Linda Baldwin (Scott) and her brothers, Rick and Mark Baldwin, share a pleasant, memorable moment with Santa Bill in 1956. *Linda Scott Private Collection.*

Opposite: An excited four-year-old, Connie Harter (Burton), visits with the Real Santa, who greeted her by name in 1955 in Santaland. *Connie Harter Burton Private Collection.*

Connie Harter Burton is in total agreement that her visit with Santa was a wonderful and magical time. She wrote that her dad made certain her black patent leather shoes were shiny and ready to wear for her 1955 meeting with him when she was four years old. "I remember Santa surprised me and said, 'Connie, you will get that doll baby!' Oh, the excitement on my face!"[95]

In 1949, at age seven, Frances Broaddus-Crutchfield made the visit to Miller & Rhoads with her family. She, too, recalled sweet memories of her meeting with Santa. Her encounter included a very special message from the Jolly Old Elf, as evidenced in her photo taken with him. "Santa told me a 'Christmas Secret,'" she smiled. "I promised him I would not tell it, and I never have told anyone. I have kept the secret sixty-four years!" (Ms. Broaddus-Crutchfield later was an "elf" in Santaland in the 1970s.)[96]

Of course, no matter what one wished for at Christmastime, as a recipient of Santa's generosity when he rewarded good behavior, it was imperative that he knew one's exact location on Christmas Eve. If little ones were visiting Grandma and Grandpa in Beckley, West Virginia, which was sometimes the case for me and my sister, Judy, in the early 1950s, then we wanted Santa to know that we would not be at our home in Portsmouth, Virginia, that holiday season. Also, if the family had moved sometime between one Christmas and another, it was crucial to inform Santa and his elves about the change of address.

Jane Osborne Johnson was very concerned about her move from one apartment to another in Richmond in 1949. She wrote:

Top: Frances Broaddus-Crutchfield listens as Santa Bill reveals to her a secret that she has kept, at his request, for sixty-four years, since 1949. *Frances Broaddus-Crutchfield Private Collection.*

Left: Jane Nelson Osborne (Johnson) enjoys a sweet moment with the Real Santa at Miller & Rhoads in 1949. *Jane Osborne Johnson Private Collection.*

From 1946 to 1953, my parents and I lived in apartments at 4309 Grove Avenue: first in #2, a one-bedroom apartment on the first floor, then in #6, a two-bedroom on the second floor directly above #2. We made the move upstairs sometime in 1949, I was being very concerned that Santa would deliver my presents to the wrong apartment, and mentioned this to Santa (I have no idea what I requested for Christmas.) After our conversation, I was taken to his left into what I remember as an office with a window. I told the lady standing behind the desk our address with the new apartment number and she carefully wrote it down assuring me that it would be given to Santa. (I was a young adult away from Richmond before I ever encountered anyone in a service profession who did not treat me as if dealing with me was the most important thing they had to do all day.) I also remember telling my mother that the Santa at Thalhimers was just a Santa's helper.[97]

Children from Richmond, Virginia, and youngsters from all over the commonwealth made the pilgrimage to the downtown Miller & Rhoads and the seventh floor where Santa held court. But folks of all ages came from far and wide to visit with this amazing Santa Claus.

One interested and curious but well-mannered little fellow made the trip up to Richmond from Wilmington, North Carolina, on an annual Christmas visit with his family that was a tradition for several years in the 1950s. Joe Pace, still a Wilmington resident, has a remarkable memory and has savored through the years his vivid recollections of his visits to Richmond at Christmas and, most specifically, Miller & Rhoads.

I think my first visit was at age nine, which would have been in 1956, and a second visit the next year in 1957. Anyway, it was a very exciting time as my mother took me and my younger brother, George, who would have been age five at the time in 1956, to see Santa. We went in the morning, right after breakfast at the John Marshall Hotel, where we were staying. We wanted to get there early to avoid some of the crowds of people that Mother said would be there, so we would not have to stand so long in line.

As to what I recall about the décor of "Santaland" is as follows, and it may not be exactly right as to how the room looked, but this is what I have stored in my mind…The room was of a fairly large size (at least to a small boy), but I don't really remember it seeming to be real big. As you entered from what I called the back of the room, you could see a very well-lighted area in the front that had a very nice chair for the Snow Queen, a beautiful Christmas tree, a large throne-like chair where Santa sat, and a fireplace that had some kind of Christmas decorations on the mantelpiece, I think. The room also had some rows of chairs where people sat to either wait to visit Santa or to watch children visiting Santa. I guess this may have been where the parents sat. This part of the room had lighting, but was kind of dark or what I might call dimly lit. I know the story is that Santa came down the chimney to enter the room each day, but I never saw that happen, so I have to the take the good word that it did. This is my best recollection of "Santaland."

I remember us being in a line, but it was not too long, and it seemed to move along. We did pretty well on our timing, as when it was our turn, my brother and I walked up to see the Snow Queen first, and then in a few minutes, we went over to sit on Santa's legs. I was amazed when Santa called my name and the name of my younger brother. That was very impressive and like, hey, this must be the real one, because he knows our names! I remember I asked for a couple of cars to add to my train set I had gotten several years earlier, and I think I asked for a set of switch tracks. I know I did not ask for very many items, as my mother had told me he was a very busy man and had a lot of work to do to get all the stockings filled. I also told Santa about how much I liked my train and that just a few things to add would be very nice. I also remember him pointing to the camera so we would be looking in the right direction for our pictures to be made. Another thing I remember was a little sign board on a stand right beside Santa that had a number on it and some other writing. I guess this was a system they must have used to keep track of the pictures being made. That is about it for the Santa visit, but there was more later in the day that we did not know at the moment was coming.

When it was time for lunch about midday, my mother said we were going to the Tea Room and have lunch, and that we would see Santa and the Snow Queen and we would be able to have lunch with them. Sure enough, when we got off the elevator at the Tea Room floor, there were lots of people and lines coming out of the dining room. My mother told us to get in the line for three and stay there. We did and the line moved along and before long, we had a table very close to the end of the steps that lead to a platform and stage area. Not very long after we sat down for our lunch, the Snow Queen and Santa came out on the stage and sat at a long table at the front. We all ate our meals and enjoyed it. There was a fashion show of ladies walking around on the stage and platform modeling clothes. They would also come down the steps near us and walk around the dining room. After Santa finished his lunch, it was announced that all the boys and girls

Miller & Rhoads' "Poll-Parrot's" comic book, a probable Christmas souvenir from Santaland, 1951. *Lewis Parks Private Collection.*

The Toy Department was a busy place for customers and store employees at Miller & Rhoads in downtown Richmond at Christmas, circa 1953. *Photo by Flournoy. Courtesy Virginia Chamber of Commerce, Valentine Richmond History Center.*

should come to a table near the foot of the steps and get a slice of Rudolph Cake from Santa. As luck would have it, this table was just one table over from where we were sitting, so we did not have far to go to get our cake, which was pretty in colors of white, green, and red icing. As I remember, it was white on the inside and tasty!

One of the other things that sticks out in mind about our visit that day was sometime during the afternoon. We got to the toy department where the trains were located in the store. I never will forget all the wonderful train engines, cars and accessories they had on display that you could add to your train set. It was just unbelievable all the nice things they had, and naturally, I found the things I asked Santa for and pointed them out to my mother. I don't remember her saying very much about any of them, except that she thought they were nice.

Needless to say, this was a wonderful lunch and day at Miller & Rhoads. We were in the store just about the entire day from what I can remember. My mother looked at a lot of things from one floor to another. I remember after lunch that day, she wanted to shop in the Christmas shop, which was right next door to the Tea Room. She told my brother and I to find a chair outside and to sit there and be quiet and wait for her. She told us the Christmas shop had many very nice Christmas ornaments in it and we should consider it a "Don't Touch" shop; therefore, it would be best for us to stay outside of the shop and sit in some chairs nearby, which we did. She did do some shopping as she came out with the packages in hand. A wonderful day at Miller & Rhoads. We stayed until time to go back to the hotel to have supper with my father.

So, my parents had everything they enjoyed in easy walking distance from the John Marshall, and my brother and I had the wonderful visits to Miller & Rhoads to the toy department, visits with Santa, and the wonderful meals in the Tea Room.

Well, as it turned out, when Christmas rolled around back home in Wilmington, North Carolina, Santa brought me the two train cars I had asked for and the set of switch tracks. He also brought a few other small accessories that I had not asked for but that went very well with my train set. I guess when I got up on Christmas morning and found the Lionel train items I had asked for under the Christmas tree, it was a time for a confirmation for my belief in Santa. There is no telling what was going through my mind that Christmas Day. Santa is mystical and magical, and I hope none of us ever stop believing. It was all so exciting that we got to do it all over again the next year.

our Christmas bells peal out again . . .

its Christmastime at Miller & Rhoads!

The Christmas spirit is everywhere and bells are ringing in the happiest season of all! M&R is brimming with all the many things everyone dreams of finding under Christmas trees. Come see! Shop early! Use our convenient Mail Shopping Service!

Bring the children to see our Christmas windows, to meet Santa Claus in his beautiful Wonderland, and see the hilarious "King of Clowns" and his pet pig from Ringling Bros. Circus (here after Thanksgiving Day).

In addition to our many customer services we have an exclusive, beautiful Gift Wrap Service for special occasions and seasons for only 35c and 50c. As always, there is our standard gift-wrapping at no charge. If you can't decide on a gift, just give a M&R Gift Certificate redeemable in our store for whatever gift is wished at the specified amount. Send check, money order or we'll charge to your account.

And a Merry Christmas to you all!

Miller & Rhoads

THE Shopping Center
Richmond, Virginia

Miller & Rhoads Christmas catalogue, inside front page, 1950. *Lewis Parks Private Collection.*

I have often marveled and tried to figure out how my parents got all the Santa Claus and Christmas gifts purchased at Miller & Rhoads and got it all back home without my brother and me finding out about it. We never took the car out of the garage at the John Marshall Hotel once we checked in, and I don't remember ever seeing many packages in the trunk of the car. I think my mother simply went completely through the store one day of the trip and bought everything needed and had it all shipped to Wilmington.

I really look back on all of it quite often in my older life and think how very fortunate we were to have had these wonderful experiences and the memories that have been left with us. Obviously, Richmond, Virginia; Miller & Rhoads; Santa Claus; Christmas; and Lionel Trains are lasting treasures in my life. Who could possibly ask for anymore than these wonderful joys that I have experienced in my life![8]

Another family, the Nordans, did not travel quite as far as the Pace family. The destination during the 1950s for young Clyde Nordan and his parents and siblings, who were from Portsmouth, Virginia, was downtown Richmond. Usually they made the trip just for the day, and Nordan said it was always a treat to behold all the sights and sounds representative of such a joyous time. It was always interesting and exciting to see what Richmond was doing a bit differently than the Tidewater area when it came to seasonal festivities. Unfortunately, he and his family never visited with the Real Santa at Miller & Rhoads, but they saw the beautiful and elaborate M&R and Thalhimers window displays, which, by themselves, were worth the trip from Hampton Roads. He recalled that every time his family made the trek to Richmond, "it always seemed to snow, as we made our way 'north.'"

Thinking back, Nordan still likes to reminisce about his childhood Christmases and the sweetness and simplicity of that era with his nostalgic list:

Christmas of Yesterday

Mom's love of the season and decorating and making it special.
Dad's over decorating all the bushes with lights.
Decorating the tree with antique ornaments.
Electric Trains around the tree.
Apples, Tangerines, Oranges, Pecans and Walnuts.
Riding through the neighborhoods, admiring the decorations and lights.
(The low-rent areas had the best)
Ice skating
Egg Nog, or the making of same.
Fruit Cake. Love the homemade ones.
Visiting the Live Manger Scenes.
Christmas Parades and Santa.
My dad's deviled eggs. Out-of-this-world.
Hanging stockings (with care)
The Light Show by the lake out at the G.E. plant in Suffolk.

Christmas morning
in 1950 with Gail
Patterson (Brookings)
and her "doll babies"
at Grandma's in
Roanoke, Virginia.
*Gail Patterson Brookings
Private Collection.*

Christmas lights along High Street. You could barely make out the traffic signals.
Window displays in Richmond.
Coleman's Nursery.
Shooting down Mistletoe from the trees with a .22.
Receiving packages in the mail from our cousins in NC & NJ.
Hard candy in a box with a string. Hated the clove flavored.
Grapefruit for breakfast with red & green sprinkles.
Waiting for Grandma at the bus station. She always brought a suitcase full
of homemade sausage.
Train layouts at Sears and Swartz.
Before they cut it out, the displays at the Navy shipyard.
Putting luminaries at the church walk.
Making Christmas cards.

Making S'mores.
Making gifts to take to the nursing homes.
Performing in Christmas plays at elementary school.
Pollyanna
The madhouse when everybody is opening family presents.
Powdered sugar Italian Wedding cookies.
Staying up all night, putting together bikes and dollhouses.[99]

Of course, snowfalls at Christmastime are every child's "icing on the cake" to make dreams even more enticing during the holidays. Whether in Virginia or another location for seasonal celebrating, snowflakes, icicles, snowmen and hot chocolate always made December seem more like Christmas.

Spending her early years in Cranbury, New Jersey, before moving to Williamsburg, Virginia, Dottie Chermak Mears recalled those 1950s winter days of her childhood:

I remember many white Christmases when growing up in Cranbury, New Jersey. Dad would always say, "I'll take your picture in front of the house before you go out back with your sled." My brother, Bill, and I always enjoyed riding our sleds in the backyard. Mom would always remind us to come in when our fingers and toes got cold. Big snows always made Christmas even more magical![100]

That nostalgia of years gone by, especially during the season of brightly colored packages, glowing Christmas trees and warm get-togethers of family and friends, still lingers and tugs at the heartstrings.

Sandra Trott Riddell expressed her fondest thoughts about those times that still somehow never leave us. In a message, she wrote:

As I get older, I find that my memories of Richmond Christmas holidays especially in the 1950s (and later in the 1960s) are like best friends: they are safe havens of security bathed in love and happy moments with beloved family members who have passed on. A thirty two year career as a public school educator taught me that mine was a blessed childhood, and surely one that was the exception, not the norm. Born into a working class family, my parents had meager means to support my brother and I. We were not rich, but we always possessed those things that were the most important and could not be purchased with money.

Snow always makes Christmas magical, as in this wistful snow scene image featuring Dottie Chermak (Mears) at home in Cranbury, New Jersey, at Christmastime, circa 1950s. *Tom and Dottie Mears Private Collection.*

My first recollection of Christmas was in 1956, when I was three years old. On Friday nights after Thanksgiving, we bundled up against the cold and traveled from our suburban Henrico County bungalow to press our noses into the magical Miller and Rhoads and Thalhimers department store windows. We annually joined the throng of Richmonders who waited in line and visited the "real" Santa at the downtown Miller and Rhoads store. I found a very candid 1956 photo after my parents passed away, and was astounded to discover that my baby brother and I were in the presence of Santa Bill Strother, a legendary Hollywood celebrity. Somehow Santa knew just which Tiny Tears doll I wanted that year, because that little 12 inch baby miraculously appeared on Christmas morning in doll crib by the tree. Tiny Tears is still a part of this sixty-year old's life, seated in a place of honor at my home.

There was always an abundance of wonderful food for the holidays. My favorite was Christmas cookies. My Mom and her best friend would make

The Real Santa greets Sandra Trott (Riddell) and John Trott in Santaland at Miller & Rhoads, 1956. *Sandra Trott Riddell Private Collection.*

Opposite: Sandra Trott (Riddell) and cousin Tommy Collier spend time together during the holidays in Richmond, Virginia, in 1956. *Sandra Trott Riddell Private Collection.*

cookies using a cream cheese, flour and sugar recipe. This cookie dough was placed in a cookie press to become pink and white candy canes and green wreaths with cinnamon "red hots" inserted at the top. These yummy treats were stored in a candy tin and hidden away in a cabinet above the refrigerator, way out of reach of our little hands until their official unveiling on Christmas Day.

Our traditions were all family-related. On Christmas morning, we would dress up in our newest Christmas finery and visit my Grandparents' house, where there were gifts for us all as well as my Grandmother's fantasy fudge. My Grandmother used red satin ribbon to tie up her packages for us, and finished them off with very special handmade tags imported from Germany. As career antique dealers, my Grandparents would come across extraordinary things in their travels. One year they had a full-sized red *sleigh in their Highland Park living room, filled with beautifully hand wrapped packages. My Grandfather kept a set of polished brass sleigh bells hanging on the wall, which he would shake frequently to remind us that Santa was watching and that we should strive to be "good" little children. I always loved to visit my Aunt's house in the city on Christmas night, where her tree had the most glorious green bubble lights, which fascinated me for hours. The longer I observed them, the faster the bubbles moved. To this day, the smell of pine and spruce is the spark that brings back all of my best childhood Christmas memories.*

If wishes were real and dreams could come true, I want to be that little kid once again and celebrate a "home-style" family Christmas full of the excitement and anticipation that we had in the 1950s and 1960s.[101]

The dream-like memories of Miller & Rhoads at Christmas include downtown twinkling lights; whimsical and reverent store display windows; festive interior displays featuring beautiful, elaborate decorations; bustling shoppers with large "M&R" logo shopping bags bearing toys and gifts; the ever-popular Tea Room on the fifth floor; and of course, the seventh floor where Santa, his Snow Queen and Mischievous Little Elf greeted children of all ages from the day after Thanksgiving to Christmas Eve.

Bill Deekens of Midlothian, Virginia, remembered his anticipation of visiting downtown Richmond with his family from nearby Petersburg. He said he and his older brother, Andy, especially looked forward to visiting Miller & Rhoads and Santa Claus, along with all the other sights and sounds of Christmas in the 1950s.

My first recollection of visiting with Santa Claus was as a four year old child back in the mid-1950s. It wasn't until a few years later that I realized that the "Real Santa" could only be visited by going to the Miller & Rhoads department store. Growing up in Petersburg, Virginia, it was a much anticipated annual event. Along with my older brother, Andy, as well as Mom & Dad, we would pile into the car to make the twenty-five mile journey to Richmond. The excitement began to grow when we spotted the beacon that then shined atop the Medical College of Virginia Hospital, then the tallest building in Richmond (and where I was born!) and only a couple of blocks east of Miller & Rhoads.

Dressed in our Sunday best, our first stop would always be at the corner of Fifth & Grace Streets to marvel at the electric train sets that always adorned the store's corner windows. For two young boys, this was a marvelous display

Downtown Richmond's M&R Jewelry Department, located on the first floor, was packed with mostly gentlemen shoppers circa 1954—perhaps Christmas Eve! *Courtesy Valentine Richmond History Center.*

and worthy of many long stares. Next, it was inside the store and off to the escalators, never the elevators. Who wanted to ride a boring elevator, when you could be riding up five floors of moving stairs? At the fifth floor, we would eagerly, but likely not very patiently, wait in line for our turn to be seated in the Tea Room and await the arrival of Santa and his beautiful Snow Queen. I am sure we enjoyed dinner too, but that memory just fades away when compared to all of the excitement going on all around us—Santa's arrival; the lovely Snow Queen's grand entrance; Santa drinking his milk and encouraging all the boys and girls to do so as well; Eddie Weaver playing all our favorite Christmas music on the organ and, of course, getting up close to Santa to receive our slice of Rudolph Cake.

Next, it was back to the escalators to ascend two more floors for our actual visit with Santa. Unfortunately, it also meant another impatient wait as there were always many other children already in line—and waiting to do the exact same thing. The line gradually shortened as we snaked our way

Top: Brothers Andy (left) and Bill Deekens play with their toys and their dad, Stewart Deekens, on Christmas morning in 1955, at their home in Petersburg, Virginia. *Bill and Donna Strother Deekens Private Collection.*

Left: Andy, Bill and their mom, Fannie Deekens, visit with Santa Bill at Miller & Rhoads in 1953. *Bill and Donna Strother Deekens Private Collection.*

~ *Virginia Cardinal and Dogwood* ~

Miller & Rhoads Tea Room menu cover, 1950. *Lewis Parks Private Collection.*

back and forth through the Santaland rails. Finally, our view of Santa, the Snow Queen, Santa's Elf and all the decorations slowly improved. Almost without exception, it seemed that as we got to the final row in line, Santa would need to "Go up on the roof and check on the reindeer." We later realized that a bath room break was in order. Or, even perhaps a wardrobe adjustment, necessitated by a child getting a bit too excited may have also

APPETIZERS

FRESH ORANGE JUICE	.15
CHILLED TOMATO JUICE	.15
SHRIMP COCKTAIL	.35 AND .60
OYSTER COCKTAIL	.30

SOUPS

	Cup	Bowl
HOME MADE CLAM CHOWDER	.15	.25
HOME MADE VEGETABLE SOUP	15	25

CHEF'S QUICK SPECIAL

90

Wooden Salad Bowl of Julienne Ham, Cheddar Cheese,
Tomato Wedges, Water Cress, Mixed Greens and
Celery in Cup of Crisp Lettuce, Special
Blend French Dressing, Rolls

DIET LUNCHEON SPECIAL

FRUITED COTTAGE CHEESE ON BED OF SHREDDED LETTUCE,
SLICED PEACHES, ONE HARD ROLL, BLACK COFFEE
OR TEA WITH LEMON 70

PLAIN OMELETTE, QUARTERED TOMATOES, CREAMED
POTATOES, SLICED PEACHES, ONE SLICE OF WHOLE
WHEAT BREAD, BLACK COFFEE OR BUTTERMILK . . 1.00

SALADS & SALAD BOWLS

CHICKEN SALAD, VEGETABLE SALAD, DEVILED EGGS,
SARATOGA CHIPS 95

GULFPORT SALAD, FRESH LOBSTER MEAT, CRAB, SHRIMP,
HARD COOKED EGGS, TOMATO WEDGES, SARATOGA
CHIPS, CRISP PICKLE 1.10

A FRESH PINEAPPLE RING WITH ASSORTED FRESH FRUITS,
TOPPED WITH FLUFFY ORANGE DRESSING 85

TOMATO FILLED WITH FRESH SHRIMP ON CRISP LETTUCE,
CARRROT STICKS 1.00

SALAD OF VINEGARED BEETS, CARROTS, CABBAGE AND
PEPPER SALAD, TOMATO SLICES, COTTAGE CHEESE,
ASPARAGUS TIPS 60

FROZEN FRUIT SALAD, DAINTY SANDWICHES 75

SLICED PINEAPPLE ON CRISP LETTUCE, GRATED AMERICAN CHEESE,
FRENCH DRESSING 60

HEART OF LETTUCE, ROQUEFORT CHEESE DRESSING . . .50

Miller & Rhoads Tea Room

RECOMMENDED BY DUNCAN HINES

TODAY'S MENU   FRIDAY, MAY 12,

SHOPPERS HOT LUNCHEON

SCALLOPED HAM AND POTATOES AU GRATIN IN CASSEROLE . . .
SALISBURY STEAK, BROWN GRAVY . . . .
INDIVIDUAL DOUBLE CRUST CHICKEN PIE . . . .
ROAST LEG OF LAMB WITH DRESSING AND GRAVY . . . .

NEW POTATO, PARSLEY BUTTER   SCALLOPED EGG PLA
BROCCOLI, HOLLANDAISE SAUCE   CORN ON C
PINEAPPLE, CARROT, AND COTTAGE CHEESE SALAD

(The price of each Entree includes 2 Vegetables, Bread and Butter)
Tea, Coffee or Milk

SPECIAL LUNCHES

VEGETABLE PLATE—BOILED KALE AU GRATIN POTATOES, BLACKEYE
PEAS, STEWED TOMATOES . . . .

WELSH RAREBIT IN CASSEROLE, TOAST POINTS, CRISP BACON,
GREEN PEAS COLESLAW . . . .

CREAMED CHICKEN AND SWEETBREADS IN PASTRY SHELL, CORN ON
COB, TOSSED VEGETABLE SALAD . . . .

Tea, Coffee or Milk served with above.

SEA FOOD SPECIALTIES

FRESH CRAB FLAKES AU GRATIN IN CASSEROLE, BOILED
KALE, SQUASH . . . .

FRIED VIRGINIA SHAD, BOILED KALE, CREAMED POTATOES . . .

COMBINATION FISH PLATE—SHRIMP COCKTAIL, CRAB CAKE, BROILED
FISH, SALMON SALAD, QUARTERED TOMATOES, DUCHESSEE
POTATOES . . . .

★MILLER AND RHOADS DEVILED CRAB, TARTAR SAUCE, CHOICE OF
TWO VEGETABLES OR TOMATO ASPIC AND COLESLAW . . .

Tea, Coffee or Milk served with above.

Orders Taken For Decorative Cakes, Wed ¯ gs, Birthdays and Special Occasions A
Hostess Cake Box on First Floor

★Star indicates items which may be purchased to take home. It will be prepared wh
you are having lunch.

We accept reservations for special occasions, bridal showers, birthday parties and
parties, from 2:00 to 5:00 P. M.

Miller & Rhoads Tea Room menu, inside, 1950. *Lewis Parks Private Collection.*

been involved, thus leaving an unexpected present in Santa's lap! For years
afterward, my Mother would always love to repeat the story of how I
would always say to her when Santa announced that he needed to check
on the reindeer and would be "back in five minutes!" As a little fellow, I
would repeat out loud to everyone within ear-shot Santa's announcement,
"Santa Claus will be back in five minutes." I am sure that over the next five
minutes, I would ask repeatedly, if five minutes was up yet!

Finally, our turn would come and we got to hear Santa call us by name,
and it was truly amazing! He always remembered our names. After visiting
with him, having our picture taken and, of course, telling him what we

SANDWICHES

EEF BRISKETS ON RYE BREAD .40   HAM .40

E SANDWICH ON WHOLE WHEAT BREAD .25

CLUB SANDWICH .70   JUNIOR CLUB .50

TOMATO AND BACON SANDWICH .40

SALAD .50   EGG SALAD SANDWICH .30

CHEESE .45   PASTROMI SANDWICH .50

CHICKEN SANDWICH .60

DESSERTS

AWBERRY SHORTCAKE, WHIPPED CREAM .25

RED CHERRY ICE CREAM TART .20

AD AND BUTTER PUDDING, RAISIN SAUCE .15

EMON SPONGETTE, WHIPPED CREAM .20

SLICED PEACHES WITH CREAM .15

CREAM—VANILLA, CHOCOLATE, LEMON .15

FRUIT, LEMON MILK SHERBET .15

CARAMEL PECAN, STRAWBERRY .20

PINEAPPLE SUNDAE .25

BUTTERSCOTCH CRUNCH SUNDAE .25

ocolate, Butter Pecan, Coffee, Peppermint. Qt. 89c   Pt. 45c

BEVERAGES

*1 DAIRY MILK .10   ICE CHOCOLATE .15

OCOLATE .15   FILSON CLUB COFFEE .10

NGE PEKOE TEA .10   COCA-COLA .10

UTTERMILK .10   GINGERALE .10

would like to charge your luncheon to your account
ase present your Charga-Plate to the waitress.

onsible for clothing or packages, when not checked.
Free check room in Foyer.

wanted for Christmas, it was suddenly all over for another year. Mentally exhausted, I am confident that the trip home, although it only took about 45 minutes, involved sleep, and no doubt sweet dreams. It was a beautiful, nostalgic time from my childhood that, to this day, I still fondly recall and cherish, especially when the Christmas holidays roll around![102]

Little tykes and their families often enjoyed lunch or dinner in the Tea Room. The huge destination location (it could seat up to eight hundred diners), was a charming and delightful location for anyone who wanted to dine on signature culinary dishes such as the Missouri Club, Turkey Pot Pie, Frozen Fruit Salad and Chocolate Silk Pie. The restaurant was the go-to place in the 1940s and '50s for ladies who donned their latest hats and gloves, businessmen who conversed in the "Stag Corner" and everyone who enjoyed the many fashion shows presented by lovely models. The newest fashions were paraded on the runway by the models' presentations, enhanced even more by the merry tunes played on the Hammond organ and the piano by the ever-entertaining Eddie Weaver.

But at Christmas, the Tea Room truly belonged to Santa Claus. For the folks who could not catch his show in Santaland, or even for those who did visit with him or planned to do so on the seventh floor, the Tea Room afforded another opportunity to experience his magic of the season.

Beginning in the 1940s, "Rudolph cake" was distributed personally by Santa to the children who were dining in the Tea Room. He handed out cuts of the Christmas cake—specially made by his famous reindeer, Rudolph—to excited youngsters (aided by parents of the very little ones who needed assistance). In those days, Santa Bill made a point to offer a short, informal prayer prior to his "cutting the cake." Part of the routine of the entertainment included the appearance of Felix the Clown and his real little pig sidekick, Amelia. Felix was a professional Ringling Brothers Barnum &

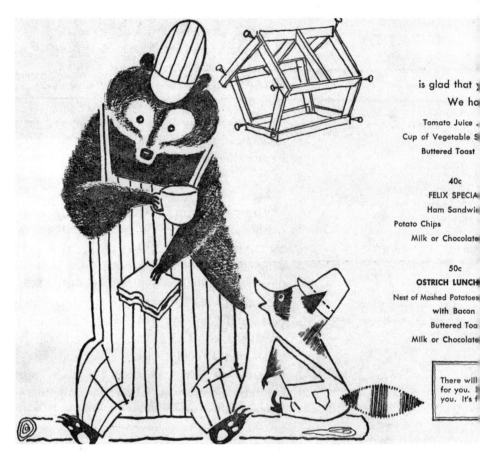

Miller & Rhoads Tea Room children's Christmas menu, inside, 1956. *Lewis Parks Private Collection.*

Bailey Circus clown who took leave in 1946 from his usual traveling circus route at Christmas and began working at Miller & Rhoads as an extra holiday attraction. He and Amelia (plus an earlier piglet named Shirley) played the Christmas season at the store from 1946 to 1956.[103]

According to a biography by Anne Aull Bowbeer, Felix the Clown and Shirley began working at Miller & Rhoads on Monday, December 2, 1946.

> *It happened that some employees of the Richmond department store, Miller & Rhoads, went to see the big show* [the Ringling Brothers Barnum & Bailey Circus at their Richmond, Virginia, engagement]. *They were so impressed by the clowns that they determined to get one to*

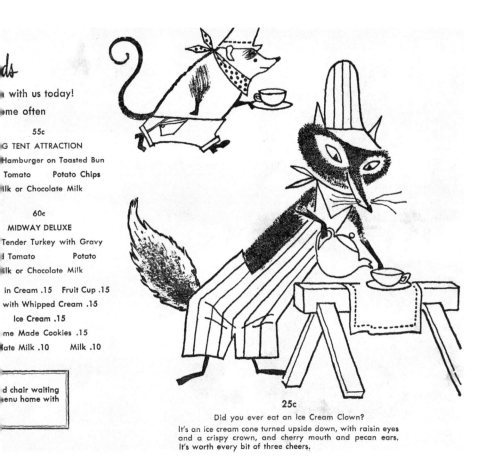

with us today!
me often

55c
G TENT ATTRACTION
Hamburger on Toasted Bun
Tomato   Potato Chips
lk or Chocolate Milk

60c
MIDWAY DELUXE
Tender Turkey with Gravy
d Tomato   Potato
lk or Chocolate Milk

in Cream .15   Fruit Cup .15
with Whipped Cream .15
Ice Cream .15
me Made Cookies .15
late Milk .10   Milk .10

d chair waiting
enu home with

25c
Did you ever eat an Ice Cream Clown?
It's an ice cream cone turned upside down, with raisin eyes
and a crispy crown, and cherry mouth and pecan ears,
It's worth every bit of three cheers,

perform in the store during the Christmas season. Their Santa Claus was already so successful that 75,000 people came to see him each year. When the employees approached Felix about locating a clown, Felix said, "What about me?"[104]

Felix and Shirley became popular attractions at the store. (Shirley was a piglet that had been named for Felix's then girlfriend, a bareback rider). But in 1949 at Christmas, Felix came back to Miller & Rhoads for the fourth year at Christmas. According to Bowbeer's biography on Adler, Felix brought with him a new sidekick, Amelia the Pig. Bowbeer wrote:

Christmas at M & R

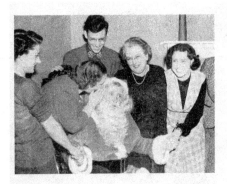

Old Saint Nick visited M & R again this year and a wonderful Santa he was, too. The twinkle in his eye had lost none of its glow; his white beard shone even whiter; and employees paid their visit along with Brother and Baby Sis, to whisper their Christmas wishes in his ear.

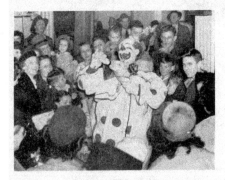

Creating mirth, laughter, and wonderment as he sojourned through the store, Felix Adler, the King of Clowns with Barnum and Bailey Circus, kept parents and employees, as well as small tots in a constant state of amusement during his stay here . . . His pint-size porker, Shirley, stole the show.

Many a small heart beat faster this Christmas when they looked over the wonders of our Toy Department with unbelieving eyes. A land of magic for little folks, trains, dolls and games spelled squeals of joy, come Christmas morning. They were waiting for Santa . . . and hoping!

The *Mirror*, Miller & Rhoads' employee newsletter of December 1946, featured highlights of that Christmas season: Santa Bill, Felix and Shirley and the Toy Department. *Penn Burke Private Collection.*

With him was his newest pig, "Amelia," (named for Felix's "new wife," Richmond native Amelia Irvin). "Amelia the Pig" was reported to be a purebred white Poland China that he picked up in Memphis at the end of October when she was a week old. At that time she could fit in Felix's pocket. By the Miami stand three weeks later, November 22–25, Amelia was ready to perform. Because of fire regulations, Felix was not allowed to do a stationary act, which would have drawn a crowd; he and the pig essentially did a walk-around through the department store. While strolling around Miller & Rhoads, the porcine Amelia wore a "jaunty" straw hat, bright red leash, and nail polish on her hooves. When not on stage, "spareribs" Amelia rested in a straw-filled pen in Felix's dressing room. Her half-sister, who had performed with Felix the year before, now weighed 380 pounds, Felix said. Felix had already picked out the pig's Richmond retirement home, the O.W. Mallory farm, where her half-sister lived.[105]

At the Miller & Rhoads' Tea Room show, at the time that Santa recited his prayer for the "Rudolph Cake," Felix appeared at what he considered the appropriate time—when a great crowd already had gathered—and entered triumphantly with his leashed piglet in tow. Of course, the prayer time was interrupted by the clown and his traveling companion, and the entire reverent mood was disrupted. Santa endured the upstaging, probably longer than any other performer would have tolerated, and complained to the executives that Felix and Amelia's presence was not appreciated by him, especially while he attempted to set a proper atmosphere for prayer. The piglet and the clown were banished from any appearance at that particular hour in the Tea Room. Otherwise, it was reported the two were constantly seen all over the store, and they continued as attractions at M&R throughout the 1940s and '50s.[106]

As reported in the biography *Felix Adler*, when entertaining children during Christmas seasons at Miller & Rhoads, Felix had several sure-fire gag lines:

Usually he fed his pig milk with a baby's bottle and allowed children to do so also. His gag line—"Now stop it, Amelia, you're making a pig of yourself"—always sent the children into peals of laughter…

Another line children loved was in a discourse on the faults of the human body. The mouth, he said, "should be on top of the head so when you got up late you could put your breakfast in your hat and eat it on your way to school."

He usually would end the act by looking at a large alarm clock strapped to his wrist and saying, "Well, well, it's half past a quarter to and I've got to be going." Then he would be off for another part of the store.[107]

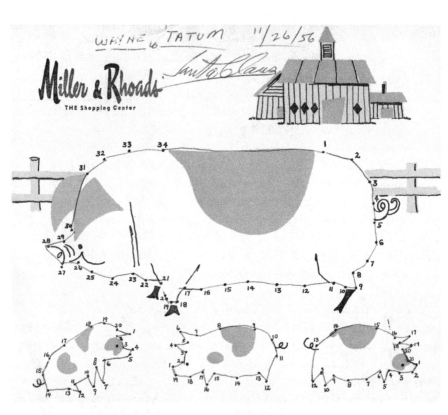

Above: Miller & Rhoads' Tea Room children's Christmas menu, back side with Santa Claus autograph, 1956. *Wayne & Lynne Tatum Private Collection.*

Left: Youngster Doug Riddell enjoys an engaging moment with Santa Bill in Santaland at the store in 1951. *Doug Riddell Private Collection.*

Another feature of the Tea Room and, indeed, a popular fixture of Miller & Rhoads downtown was the marvelous, talented musician Eddie Weaver. His nimble fingers produced exquisite music as they ran up and down keyboards of both the organ and the piano located strategically next to the Tea Room stage. He kept that post for almost fifty years and was heralded by both adults and children.

Doug Riddell remembered his good fortune to have visited with both Santa Bill and Eddie Weaver on several excursions to Miller & Rhoads when a very young lad:

I'm fortunate enough to have occupied the lap of Santa Bill Strother at least five or six times before his time at Miller & Rhoads ended. I've come up with two pictures of myself—one, very rare—in which he posed with his hat on. I'm told by the author that this was very unusual, because Miller & Rhoads Santas almost always took their red, fur-lined cap off and laid it over the back of their chair. From the look on his face though, it must have been a long *day, or I had tested his patience.*

While I was among the kids who came to Miller & Rhoads to confide my wants to the "real" Santa, my trips to the downtown store were motivated by my desire to see the magic world of model trains in the storied Fifth and Grace Streets display window, as well as to watch the legendary Eddie Weaver perform his magic on the keyboard of the Hammond electronic organ and the spinet piano that was placed perpendicular to it. This enabled the talented musician to play both simultaneously, while often blending in a third tune using both of his feet on the pedals of the Hammond. Not an easy trick for anyone.

I'd made up my mind early in life that I wanted to learn to play the organ, and often rushed up to the organist at our church, at the conclusion of the Sunday worship service, to marvel at the twinkling indicator lights, the black and ivory keys and the vibration of the bass pedals. Watching Eddie Weaver perform on the huge Wurlitzer pipe organ at downtown Richmond's Loew's Theatre was even more thrilling, so when my annual trek to the Miller & Rhoads Tea Room arrived each Christmas season, I didn't mind waiting in line—one that stretched halfway across the store—to dine with Santa, his Snow Queen and Eddie Weaver.

At times, I think I was totally oblivious to what Santa and the Snow Queen were doing, or what my parents had ordered for me to eat, because as soon as we were shown to our table, I rushed up to the side of the fashion runway, where the instruments were located and immediately began engaging Eddie in conversation. I'm sure he didn't remember me, but then, I was so persistent, I'm sure I stood out. Years later, I'd get to know him a bit better, when he played the grand Wurlitzer at Richmond's Byrd Theater. If he recalled the annoying little brat that used to hop up on the bench of the Hammond organ beside him at the Tea Room, he never let on. I never ever touched the keys, and it was for certain that my feet were never ever long enough to reach the pedals.

For me, it wasn't Christmas without my annual visit to see the real Santa at Miller & Rhoads. Although he never did bring me the organ I so badly wanted and asked for, he did remember to leave me a train of some kind almost every year. Looking back on it, one out of two isn't bad, is it?[108]

Eddie Weaver especially enjoyed playing for the many fashion shows produced by Miller & Rhoads in the Tea Room throughout the year. But at Christmas, the fashion department, in particular, embraced the season along with the rest of the store, and stunning models walked the runway in both classic and intriguing outfits to help promote the season.

Sue Ferrell was one of the models at the store during the 1950s. She recalled the fashion shows held everyday there during Christmas and her participation:

One holiday season in particular, I modeled a "Holiday House" dress to promote the "Holiday House" Christmas shop that opened to customers next to the Tea Room on the fifth floor. The dress was all green—I was dressed in it as a Christmas tree—and I wore a starred crown on top of my head that represented the star on top of a tree. The beautiful skirt of the dress had imported ornaments sewn all around it. Carol Bryson of the fashion department sewed each one on the skirt by hand. I remember some of the ornaments were intrinsic and just adorable, such as a little angel looking in a mirror; angels hanging on a half-moon; and a little white fur muff, in miniature, for one's hands. But the dress itself was made by a lady who was a seamstress, and I remember she lived on Leigh Street, not far from the store. Miller & Rhoads used her fine services on many occasions. For this particular dress, I walked to her home for the fitting.

The Christmas fashion show was held Monday through Saturday in the Tea Room, from the day after Thanksgiving until Christmas Eve day. I wore the dress on the days I worked, and another girl wore it on the other days. One of the other models I shared the dress with was Nancy Middledorfer. Whoever modeled it in the show walked out first as soon as

Santa Bill Strother and Sue Ferrell, "Miss Holiday House," pose together for a photo taken in Santaland at the store, circa 1952. *Sue Ferrell Private Collection.*

Eddie played an appropriate Christmas song. Also, I remember wearing a banner with the dress that announced "Miss Holiday House."

One day after a show, I was asked by one of the store's promotions' staff, Ken Allen, to go up to the seventh floor to Santaland and have my picture made with Santa. Of course, I did what I was asked to do. I met the Real Santa, Bill Strother, at that time. The photo of the two of us was taken, and I now have a very lovely memento of our brief visit together.[109]

Although Ms. Ferrell said she never had the pleasure of working with Santa Bill, she later was a Snow Queen in the late 1950s for the Santa Train that ran from Richmond to Ashland. But she said she did recall that Santa Bill dined on the stage in the Tea Room at lunch time with the Snow Queen, and he was present there during her fashion shows.

A festive Miller & Rhoads Christmas window display in downtown Richmond, Virginia, featuring children's fashions and candy canes, circa 1954. *Courtesy Dementi Studios.*

"I remembered him 'drinking his milk' on stage for the children and making a real show of that before he gave out the Rudolph cake," she said. "And," she added, "I saw Felix the Clown and his pig as they paraded through the store, and that was an extra treat for the kids at Christmas as well!"[110]

One particular story she recalled regarding Santa Bill Strother was that early in the 1950s, she remembered seeing a "nicely dressed" gentleman whom she did not recognize one day in the Tea Room as he chatted with musician Eddie

Weaver. According to Ms. Ferrell, the man, dressed in his street clothes of a handsome suit, walked away after his brief talk with Weaver.

"I approached Eddie to ask him something about an upcoming fashion show and commented to him, 'Who was that gentleman?'"

"Oh, that's Santa Claus!" Weaver quickly replied. "He thinks he is '*the* Real Santa,' and he is!"

Ms. Ferrell noted that she caught a passing glimpse of Bill Strother's bright blue eyes, and she thought at the time, "He has the most beautiful blue eyes I have ever seen!"[111]

Ms. Ferrell commented that, as far as she knew, the "Holiday House" promotion only ran for that one Christmas season at the store in the early 1950s. Another elegant "Christmas Shop" took over in the same location in the ensuing years that followed.[112]

But in addition to its famous Santa Claus and the Tea Room, Miller & Rhoads offered throughout the 1940s and '50s other facets at Christmastime that attracted throngs of customers and became holiday traditions on their own merit.

The fifty-four windows that encircled the building on all four sides featured holiday themes that ran from whimsical to fantastic; historical to religious; and humorous to thought-provoking. M&R display director Addison Lewis mastered the sensational windows for more than fifty years, with many of his memorable and most productive years being in the 1940s and '50s. The Christmas windows were particularly stunning, and Lewis was aided by other talented members of his team such as Penn Montague, Allen Rhodes and Milton Burke. The displays were admired not only by Richmonders but also by people who would travel from distant cities to view them.[113] Some of Lewis's most touching displays were the Liberation Day and the Christmas Prayer windows, both during World War II.[114] Special commemorative booklets were published as companion pieces made available to customers.

The late Milton Burke, often referred to as "Mr. Miller & Rhoads," devoted forty-three years to his job at the retailer, beginning in the 1940s. He assisted in all display tasks, and his creative touches could be seen throughout the store, which included his decorations in Santaland. In particular, his flair was recognizable in the impressive floor and window displays. Along with the tireless efforts of Burke and others on the display teams, offerings such as the joyful "eye-candy" windows most especially helped to heighten the anticipation of Christmas for all who ventured downtown.[115]

In addition to the store happenings at Broad and Sixth Streets, Miller & Rhoads participated in other Christmas festivities in the 1940s, '50s

Prayer Windows
Christmas
1943

Prayer for Daddy

This Christmas Day, Oh God, I pray for Daddy.
Somewhere out there is he, we know not where.
Thou knowest where he is.
Please, Lord, watch over him.
And keep him, Lord, within Thy loving care.
Tell him Thou lovest him. We love him, too.
So, Lord, I pray that Thou wilt let him know.
Please bring him safe back to me and mother.
I love my Daddy, Lord, I love him so.

Amen.

Top: Miller & Rhoads booklet *Come In, Buddy* included a section called "Prayer Windows, Christmas, 1943" that complemented the window displays. *Penn Burke Private Collection.*

Left: A poignant World War II "Prayer for My Daddy," from the M&R published booklet *Come In, Buddy,* complemented one of the store's window displays in 1943. *Penn Burke Private Collection.*

and into the '60s, most especially outdoor celebrations such as the area's annual Christmas parade. The store sponsored a sparkling holiday-themed float, adorned with many of the Miller & Rhoads' models who waved enthusiastically to the hundreds of spectators lining the streets on the parade route. The popular evening celebration began at Chimborazo Park in Church Hill and traveled west on Broad Street. M&R had a presence each year in the annual Tobacco Bowl Festival Parade as well.[116]

And thanks to the store's efforts and the eagerness of Santa to go out into the community, Miller & Rhoads continued its Christmas goodwill past the borders of downtown. Through the years that Santa Bill occupied the chair, M&R arranged numerous meetings with children who were unable to visit him in Santaland. These little ones were in hospitals or orphanages, and some were even classified as shut-ins at home and had no other recourse than to have Santa pay them a visit. Such social calls were carried out willingly and unselfishly by Santa Bill. Regarding this, Clifford Dowdey wrote in his article in the *Saturday Evening Post*, "To the shut-in children of the proper age group, he personifies a dream come true. They are more uninhibited in their responses than most children in the store, and Bill has performed some near miracles with ill and crippled children. He encourages their efforts by holding out rewards only a Santa could offer, and under his encouragement, children have walked, improved in body and changed in mental attitude."[117]

By the early 1950s, Santa Bill had his routine both at the store and in the community down pat. Putting all his efforts into the role, he sought to make his "Santy" (as he sometimes referred to himself) a year-round vocation.[118]

About 1946, Bill and Grady decided to sell the Strother House in Petersburg.[119] The war was over, and their tourist home had more vacancies. Bill was busy with the Santa appearances at the store at Christmastime, but Mrs. Strother missed the Los Angles, California area and also her sister, who had settled there. The couple decided to move back to Burbank. (The Strother House later became the property of the Petersburg General Hospital and was used as a boardinghouse for nurses. It was demolished in the mid-1950s.)

A former Miller & Rhoads executive, Tom Mitchell, lived much of his early life in Petersburg and remembered the Strother House to be a real "showcase." I was treated to a historic tour of the city by Mitchell, who enjoys giving tours of historic Petersburg, and he showed me where the house once stood on South Sycamore Street. The brick school for nurses that was built on the site of the Victorian home can be seen on the property today, but it is no longer in use. Interestingly, the beautiful original wrought-iron

MONDAYS
9 to 9

Behind the S

Above: Jackie Vial and Betty McIntosh
get under way on a large-scale
bow-tying project.

With Christmas i
go into high-gear
deer and all manne
corner in the prove
white beards—they
mannequin under c
do a wonderful job
factors in sales pro

Left: Milton Burke ac
with Christma

Above: Arthur Hood is making a chandelier drop which Betty
will transform into a thing of beauty with ornaments.

Left: Dante Santacroce and
Richard Dunn, of the Sign
Shop, rig up an easel display.

Miller & Rhoads' employee newsletter the *Mirror* featured a behind-the-scenes center spread for upcoming Christmas preparations at Richmond's downtown store in October 1951. *Penn Burke Private Collection.*

with Interior Display's Crew

ntague, Waverly Barnum and their hard-working crew
store takes on a festive appearance as Santa Clauses,
ts come out of hiding. Interior Display itself looks like a
North Pole except that the workers aren't dwarfs with long
e you see bustling about, frequently with a life-sized
outfit in the other and a festoon around the neck. They
attractive and inviting and their displays are tremendous
're super people!

Davis, who's
r mache, puts
beards on all
Clauses.

Above: Johnny Gabbert finishes his
sign under the surveillance
of the doe.

Below: Up goes a finished product in
the Stationery Department with
all hands on deck.

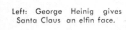
Above: Edwin Barchet puts the
finishing touches on a sign.

Left: George Heinig gives
Santa Claus an elfin face.

161

Above: Miller & Rhoads was represented in annual Christmas parades in Richmond, Virginia, especially in the 1950s. A snowflake and reindeer–themed float was featured in 1953. *Dementi photo. Sue Ferrell Private Collection.*

Left: Santa Bill Strother and his wife, Ethel "Grady" Strother, circa 1940s. *Nelson and Marilyn Strother Private Collection.*

fencing that Mitchell said was a part of the property is still prominent in the front yard. Once lovely but now neglected shrubbery and ancient-looking flowering trees still are evident. No doubt they were a part of the property long before the Strothers occupied it. What a pity historic preservationists did not act to save the lovely house from the wrecking crews in the 1950s.[120] The only photograph I discovered of the home as the Strother House was a vintage postcard from the 1940s.

So, the decision was made for Bill and Grady Strother to move to Burbank, California. In Richmond, the Santaland operation was a tremendous success, but it only ran for four weeks, from Thanksgiving to Christmas. Bill Strother so believed in his mission as Santa Claus that he considered it not only a job, but his entire purpose in life, not just in Richmond, Virginia, but wherever he was "called."[121]

One time when he visited a very ill little boy in Los Angles during the off-season, he cheered-up the child by reassuring him, "You don't have to wait until Christmas for Santy. Santa Claus lives all the time!"

So, with that philosophy and commitment, Strother and his wife moved back to California. Santa Bill spent his waking hours from January 1 to November 20—immediately following Christmas to just prior to the holidays—promoting his belief that "Santa Claus has no season."[122]

True to his word, he appeared as St. Nick for the March of Dimes drive in Los Angeles in the spring of 1951.[123] In May, he followed that project with what he considered was one of his greatest off-season victories. Santa Bill had heard that a six-year-old boy, Donny Chafin, suffered from leukemia. He had learned of the child's menacing illness through Donny's church pastor, so Santa made a visit to the boy's home. Donny confided to his mother that his greatest wish was "to ride to the North Pole with Santa," a message that she relayed to Santa during his visit. In the next few days, Santa Bill obtained permission from the Burbank Junior Chamber of Commerce to stage a ride for Donny in the "Burbank on Parade" civic celebration. Santa, in his complete Christmas outfit, rode with Donny atop the back seat in an open convertible. The boy was made a Cub Scout mascot, and Cub Scouts rode with them. Mrs. J.L. Chafin, Donny's mom, was named an honorary den mother so she could ride in the parade as well. According to the *Hayward (CA) Daily Review* of May 21, 1951, it was estimated that hundreds of thousands of folks gathered along the route to watch the many floats and bands, along with the special "Donny" automobile, that was decorated with a sign that read, "A Dream Comes True to Don—7." Spectators shouted, "Hey, Donny!" as the car passed by in the procession. Also, Santa Bill

Santa Bill acknowledges the crowd from the Santa Village float during the Tournament of Roses Parade in Pasadena, California, in January 1955. Strother, through his association with makeup artist Max Factor Jr., was chosen by Santa's Village theme park owner Glenn Holland to portray Santa for the parade. Factor created the Santa wig and beard sets for both Strother and Holland's three Santa Village parks: Sky Forest, California; Scotts Valley, California; and Dundee, Illinois. *Phillip L. Wenz Private Collection.*

presented the young lad with a gift from his Sunday school class, along with autographed photos of Hopalong Cassidy and Jack Dempsey. In addition, "many, many prayers went up for Donny along that parade route," Strother said, "and there will be a lot more tonight."[124]

Bill Strother was willing to take "his Santa" on the road anywhere at anytime—except, of course, when he was scheduled to appear at Miller & Rhoads. One such event was reported in the November 10, 1952 edition of the *North Adams (MA) Transcript.* The actual appearance of Santa Bill was held in Stamford, Vermont, at the Grange Hall during a November snowfall. The article read:

> *Strother, nationally-known exponent of the non-commercialized Christmas and non-promising Santa Claus, plies his trade four or five weeks of every year as a Santa in a Richmond, Virginia department store. Instead of*

stringing the children along with easy promises their parents can't always fulfill, Strother tells the children of the real, unselfish spirit of Christmas and encourages them to do something especially unselfish for their parents or others at Christmas. Between Christmases, he spreads the idea across the country.

Dressed in his full Santa Claus regalia, he told the Stamford children last night: "There's always the spirit of Christmas that's symbolized by Santa." He addressed about 200 children and adults on the subject: "Taking the Commercialism Out of Christmas," stressing the original religious meaning of the day. He urged a revival of the simple old-time spiritual observance of Christmas.

Mr. Strother, who is a guest at the Stamford summer home of Philip S. Hill of New York, will leave this week for Virginia where he will play Santa Claus until Christmas.

Santa Bill was well received in many locations nationwide as the Real Santa. He promoted his ideals of the spirit of Christmas, dressed in his full regalia, at any time of the year, for those willing to accept his giving spirit and his conviction to help make wishes come true for children.

One of the major plans that he endorsed was a Santa Train donated by the railroads, with gifts donated by the Kiwanis Clubs. The train would tour across the country, bringing Santa and Christmas year round. Unfortunately, this grand idea never materialized. So the suggestion was made to Miller & Rhoads by Santa Bill that he might use Richmond as his home base and operate all year long.[125]

But there were concerns for the store to consider. Using Richmond as a permanent residence for the Real Santa would tend to remove the very special aspect of holiday visits at Christmastime. Also, the idea of Santa "in residence" for more than four weeks posed logistical problems. When he was in town from Thanksgiving to Christmas, he was transported on his visits by a limousine and a police escort. Often, his waving and greeting folks from his car caused minor traffic jams.[126]

In addition, during his four-week stay in Richmond, based at Miller & Rhoads, Santa's appearances at the store created such huge crowds that two local firemen were on loan each day from the Richmond Fire Department to monitor the hundreds of people in the Old Dominion Room auditorium that was transformed into Santaland. Also, the toys presented to shut-in children when Santa made his personal visits were billed by the Santa Claus department to the store. And, the wishes that some children imagined in hopes that they would come true sometimes

Santa Bill has fun with a Miller & Rhoads employee, Arthur "Chuck" Hood, circa 1948. Hood followed Strother as the next featured Santa Claus for the store in 1957. *Carolyn Hood Drudge Private Collection, in loving memory of Frances and Art Hood.*

Opposite: The Real Santa, Bill Strother, in his prime at Miller & Rhoads department store, downtown Richmond, Virginia, in 1953. *Courtesy Dementi Studios.*

were complicated and difficult to achieve. One example was when the children from a local cerebral-palsy clinic made their sincere wish known that they would like steel railings installed at their facility—"just like the ones in Santaland"—as aids for walking. These railings were fitted in the floor, so Miller & Rhoads took on the task of erecting steel railings at the clinic, which was most appreciated by the clinic and the entire community. However, performing such a service required not only the effort of identification of a vendor but also the task of cost evaluation and implementation. The bottom line was there were limits that had to be considered for such projects.[127]

The idea of a year-round Santa, at least in Richmond, Virginia, at Miller & Rhoads, to be instituted in the 1950s never came true. Santa Bill Strother continued to visit with children and their families at the downtown store from Thanksgiving to Christmas. He was beloved and received with open arms by thousands of visitors there each Christmas season. The partnership with Santa and M&R was viewed by all as a fabulous, successful undertaking.[128]

Today, memories abound of those undeniably unforgettable Christmas visits with Santa Bill at Miller & Rhoads. Those dear, sweet times continue to live in the minds and hearts of adults today who, as children of the 1940s and 1950s, had the incredible experience of visiting with him during his tenure.

For me, my visits with this Santa seem as if they happened just yesterday and will forever be etched in my memory. I can especially recall my meeting with him in 1956, at the age of five, when my family and I made our pilgrimage to Richmond, one hundred miles away, from our home in Portsmouth, Virginia.

It was by word of mouth that we learned of the "magical experience" at the Miller & Rhoads department store in Richmond. Like so many families in the Tidewater area, we made the two-hour trip during the Christmas holidays to visit the Real Santa there. We established this tradition and continued it every year. Many folks throughout Virginia, North Carolina and other states made similar holiday excursions to Richmond.

It was a treat to make our day trip to the Capital City, usually on a Saturday. Our excitement would steadily grow as we anticipated seeing Santa Claus, the Snow Queen and the Elf. Each year, our destination was the seventh floor and Miller & Rhoads' Santaland. There, the Old Dominion Room was transformed into an enchanted world. We knew this was Santa's "home" for the holidays, and it beckoned visitors of all ages.

Most guests from previous years knew that the Santaland waiting line would be at least a two-hour wait and probably longer, especially on a Saturday. Our hearts would beat faster and faster as we inched our way in the winding line filled with little girls in crinoline dresses and little boys in Peter Pan–collared shirts and bow ties. Finally, we would arrive at the front of the line, first talking with the beautiful Snow Queen and then meeting with the bigger-than-life Santa Claus.

The wait was sometimes tiring, but it was something we knew we had to endure, for the reward was worth it: a visit with him, the Real Santa! And, how did we know he was the Real Santa? Because this Santa not only looked like the tradition of the true Jolly Old Elf, but he also made a personal connection with each child. *He knew our names* without our telling him and without our parents or anyone in the room announcing to him who we were. He always seemed to remember us from year to year. As we keenly observed, he "knew all his boys and girls," as he would say.

Many years later, I would learn from my dad that somehow he had "communicated" with the Real Santa during those childhood visits. According to Dad, it seemed in some manner that Santa, perhaps clairvoyantly, learned that our last name was Strother, which was also his last name. Dad said that Santa asked him where our Strother family line had originated. They both concurred that we were "probably related" (I have since discovered that indeed, we are related); however, to this day, I do not know how all of this discussion between my dad and Santa was carried out so discreetly during our visit. Nevertheless, I always thought how ironic it was that fifteen years later, I would become a Snow Queen at Miller & Rhoads, my maiden name being Strother and being a relative of that very famous Santa Claus.[129]

Advancing to the store's seventh floor to Santaland was like traveling up to the North Pole. It was a destination for eager ones who made their way via elevator or escalator. Santaland was *the* home of Santa Claus. We were told it was his "home away from the *real* North Pole," and to us, it was a true holiday wonderland and fantasyland, an elaborate and astonishing display that was a feast for the eyes and that made an indelible impression not only in one's memory but also in one's heart.

Santaland did evoke the idea of a fantasyland to many people, especially children. Often the décor in the room would include snowflakes glistening and stars twinkling from the ceiling. A festive holiday exhibit, often with animated figures, was tucked in a conspicuous corner to be viewed by visitors as the line wound, maze-like, through the room. Even the temperature in Santaland seemed chilly, as a blue haze effect created by the paint hues was incorporated with impressive lighting techniques. Thus, stepping into Santaland was entering into a dimension where a true sense of a "winter wonderland" became a reality. No doubt, Santa also felt at home in his temporary Christmas location. It was not the North Pole, but it was the closest thing to actually being there, and not only the children but the adults as well were captivated and fell in love as soon as they entered the shimmering, inviting chamber.[130]

Cathy Crowell Miller and her twin sister, Nancy Crowell Dorin, recalled growing up in Richmond in the 1950s and their fond memories of visiting Santa at Miller & Rhoads. Mrs. Miller wrote about her "flashback:"

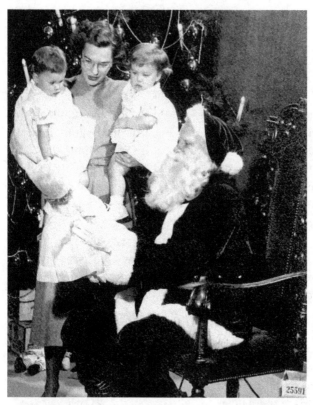

Top: Twins Cathy Crowell (Miller) and Nancy Crowell (Dorin) are held by their mom, Wanda Crowell, as they visit with Santa Bill and a doll baby in 1952. *Cathy Crowell Miller and Nancy Crowell Dorin Private Collection.*

Left: The Bendall children (left to right), Nancy (Emerson), Joan and Johnny, wait for Santa by their fireplace on Christmas Eve in 1954 in Richmond, Virginia. *Nancy Bendall Emerson Private Collection.*

I just remember waiting in "the room," and it was magical!!...My memories of long ago include our Grandmother (Nana) who would go with Mom to help with both of us. She would say that they had to leave much earlier [for downtown] *because everyone would stop her to see "those twins." We were so "adorable" when we were little...this is what Mom would tell us and I guess back then you just didn't see too many twins like you do now with all the medical miracles that they can do! Mom was so proud even to her death she was still introducing us to people as "my twins, Cathy and Nancy"...talk about embarrassing!!! Now, I would welcome it!!!*[131]

Another child of the 1950s, Nancy Bendall Emerson, remembered that time of innocence and simple faith. She wrote:

At age five, Christmas seemed to take forever to arrive. We counted the days not only to that wonderful holiday but also to our visit with Santa. Sue and I were best buddies, she with her page boy [sic] *carrot-top hair and me with poker-straight long blonde tresses, and we were going to Miller & Rhoads together to present our requests to the Jolly Old Elf himself. We each had our heart set on a different baby doll, Betsy Wetsy for Sue and Tiny Tears for me. The line to see Santa was long, and the closer we came the more nervous we became. When we finally reached that famous lap, something happened. I asked for Betsy Wetsy and Sue for Tiny Tears. We realized our mistake once the words were out, but that was too late as we were ushered to our awaiting mothers. How we worried about getting the wrong doll, not even considering that we would dare trade something brought to us by Santa. When Christmas morning arrived and my Tiny Tears sat under the tree, I realized that the great man had looked into our hearts and had granted our wishes. Such a simple toy exemplified the essence of Santa's Christmas magic.*[132]

Richmond native Rick Pearman professed that not only did Miller & Rhoads have Santa, but it also had better toys to wish for than the across-the-street competitor, Thalhimers. He and his younger sister, Janet, visited the store with their parents during the 1950s.[133] There were so many aspects of the store that they still cherish today. Janet Pearman Ralston wrote in a letter that she particularly loved the magical store windows where the elves were making toys before your very eyes. She noted that a visit with Santa was "an exciting event, but I was painfully shy and frightened of Santa...how did he know everyone's name?...and

why did I always have to sit on his lap? Yes, there was excitement, but I liked him best at a distance!" she added.

Mrs. Ralston agreed, though, that the pictures taken were priceless treasures shared with the grandmothers. "Lunch in the Tea Room was our reward afterward," she confirmed. "Our mother always ordered 'the Missouri Club' sandwich smothered in Welsh rarebit. My child's mind

Opposite: Janet Pearman (Ralston) makes certain her mother is close by as she and her brother, Rick Pearman, visit with Santa Bill in 1954. *Janet Pearman Ralston Private Collection, in loving memory of Sarah and Charles Pearman.*

Left: Colleen Covington (Simmons) expresses her Christmas wishes to Santa Bill at Santaland in 1956. *Colleen Covington Simmons Private Collection.*

imagined a Welsh rabbit, disgusting! Eddie Weaver played Christmas carols on the organ and Santa and his beautiful Snow Queen paid a visit!"[134]

Colleen Covington Simmons of Richmond reminisced in a written message about her times as a child during the Christmases of 1954, 1955 and 1956:

> *It almost makes me sad because it takes me oh so back to a wonderful time as a little girl—having lunch and reindeer cake with Santa during those sweet, youthful years. We arrived in Richmond in 1952 and I was two years old. I think I was four when Mom took me for my first visit to sit on Santa's lap and have lunch in the Tea Room! It was fabulous! And, we enjoyed it annually during the years afterwards (and my sister and I later brought our children to carry on the tradition!) Can we have a "re-do?"*[135]

Thinking back on those visits to see Santa so long, long ago, it is important to understand that at those very young, tender ages and in a more innocent, less

Santa Bill listens intently to Judith Strother (Jones) during her visit from Portsmouth, Virginia, to Miller & Rhoads in Richmond, Virginia, in 1948. *Ron and Judy Jones Private Collection.*

technologically infused era, we knew nothing about his "technique" or even questioned his authenticity. Indeed, this is the Santa we imagined and visited as children. This is the Santa with whom we fell in love. A mild-looking man, he greeted us with sincerity, integrity and a gentle, genuine nature that suggested warmth, love and charity. His soft, kind, reassuring voice bordered on being ethereal in nature. As Dowdey described, "He talked with an astonishing loquacity."[136] In today's comparison, I think of Fred Rogers of "Mr. Rogers" fame as someone who probably studied the effectiveness of such a voice. It was appropriately gentle and kind, and left an unmistakable impression. It was a voice little ones could respect. It was a voice that wide-eyed, innocent children would remember and hear again in their dreams.

As children, there was no doubt whatsoever in our hearts that yes, he was the Real Santa.

My sister, Judith Strother Jones, visited with Santa at Miller & Rhoads beginning at a very young age in 1948. By 1956, she was the big sister to me and recalled her fond memories of our visit to see Santa at M&R that Christmas season. She wrote her reflections, in verse:

Our Memories of Santa at Miller & Rhoads

Our parents started a tradition, to take in holiday sights.
And, at the top of their attractions list, Miller and Rhoads was a major delight.
My sister and I looked forward to when the holiday times rolled 'round,
Everyone showed excitement, like the circus had just come to town.

The year was 1956; I remember it so well.
Richmond draped in a blue gray sky. In the distance, one could hear the
lonely sound of a distant parish bell.
It was early in December, and we all began to shiver.
A cool, crisp, breeze had ushered in restless, discouraging, weather.

These conditions continued to linger, drifting all around,
increasing the need to cheer ourselves, with comforting thoughts and sounds.
But to our surprise, the sun came out, driving the storm away,
We were all so happy to make new plans for a warmer, sunnier day.

Mom and Dad made arrangements for us to take in the downtown sights.
Mom decided we had to wear something sensible and bright.
The dresses we wore were modest, appropriate, and sweet.
She even bought us matching hats and coats for Santa Claus to see.

Approaching the grand store's structure, we looked at the windows with glee.
There were many themes represented, from reality to fantasy.
Some displays were whimsical, while others stood alone.
Some had the feel of enchantment; others more somber in tone.

The model trains were a highlight, and a favorite among the boys.
Others enjoyed the decorations, animations and the toys.
After looking at the windows we collectively agreed,
The displays provided a holiday feast for everyone to see.

So, onward with our adventure, to seek out and explore
We gathered our strength, and courage, and went through the Miller and
Rhoads' door.
We made our way around counters, and trendy fashions galore,
Then we paused to get our bearings, and on up to the seventh floor.

My sister and I were excited about the highlight of our day.
That jolly old man we have always loved was just a short distance away.
We discovered the line for Santaland, now thinking all would be great,
only to find, that with the length of the line, we still had a good two-hour wait!

It must have been the magic in that unique Christmas space,
For the delay seemed to vanish, and the Snow Queen took its place.
She suddenly appeared at the front part of the line,
Chatting with the children, until each could share his time.

Then suddenly, my sister and I clearly heard our names.
As we turned, there was Santa beginning to exclaim, "I am so happy to see
you all, and so glad you came."
We had a nice chat; he put us right at ease.
Then, he told us how things generally happen every Christmas Eve.

He would request a glass of milk and two cookies for a treat,
And also several carrots for his Reindeer to eat.
He would remind us to be in bed before it got so late,
Then, he would ask us to pray for everybody's sake.

Santa then said, "Children, note these words, for they will make you wiser
as you grow.
Always be mindful of others, be they friend or be they foe.
Do not judge one another, but resist all evil ways. Spread love and lasting
friendships,
And keep all hatred at bay."

"Show respect to one another; give all feelings tender care,
Love, respect, and honor your parents, for you have eternal bonds to share."
With that, Santa bid adieu!
"Merry Christmas my sweet ones! I'll be seeing you."

On the way home, we all pondered the adventures of our day.
It was so much fun and such an amazing thrill!
And now, after all of these many years,
We both cherish those wonderful memories still![137]

Along with the Miller & Rhoads's commitment each Christmas, Santa Bill continued other appearances, especially in California, in the off-season. As Clifford Dowdey reported in 1957, "As they said in the Hollywood area where Strother then made his home, he was 'only terrific.' He was so wonderful that he had to be seen to be believed, and parents were eager to take their children in order that they might see him themselves."

Dowdey added that this performance, created by Bill and brilliantly executed, gave a complete illusion to children. But he said that Santa Bill insisted that the illusion was necessary to best communicate his message of "giving."[138]

Bill Strother continued his campaign of promoting the idea of a "year-round Santa" with a "Christmas in July," as well as at other times of the year. He was determined to find an avenue that would afford him the opportunity to completely devote his work—his whole being—to what he truly believed was his calling in life.

But his life would take an unimaginable and dreadful, tragic turn.

Chapter 11

END OF AN ERA, BUT THE
TRADITION LIVES ON

A ll was going well for Bill Strother. He was the famous, beloved Santa Claus not only in Virginia but also in many other cities throughout the country. He successfully appeared as the Real Santa at Miller & Rhoads in Richmond and completed his 1956 Christmas season at the landmark retailer. He gained popularity with his "off-season" holiday appearances and hoped to eventually finalize the establishment of his dream of a year-round Santa that celebrated the joy of giving, whatever the season. In short, life was good.

Then fate dealt a shocking, horrific blow. According to Annette D'Agostino Lloyd's book, *The Harold Lloyd Encyclopedia*, on Saturday, September 7, 1957, at 6:05 a.m., Strother was a passenger in a car driven by Mack S. Darnaby, the assistant fire chief of Burbank, California, where Bill and Grady Strother resided. An approaching car driven by Collie Strickland, of Burbank, drifted over the center line on U.S. Highway 6, hitting Darnaby's sedan. The seven injured parties were rushed to Antelope Valley Hospital, where William Carey Strother, age sixty-one, passed away at 7:45 a.m. He suffered severe intra-abdominal hemorrhage and multiple pelvis bone fractures. His wife, Ethel Grady Weems Strother, was badly injured in the crash. She survived but suffered from her lingering injuries until her death on September 11, 1976.[139]

A memorial service for Bill Strother was held in the Eckerman Chapel in Burbank on Friday, September 13, 1957, at 2:00 p.m. Dr. Martin L. Long officiated at the service. Mary Long served as the organist. The soloist was Grace Eckerman, who sang "In the Garden," and "The Twenty-third Psalm."[140]

Interment was in Valhalla Memorial Park, in Burbank. Bill and Grady Strother rest in Section 824, Block A, Lots 5 and 6. (It is interesting to note that the most famous "star" buried at this same Memorial Park is comedian Oliver Hardy, a contemporary of Strother in the early days of Hollywood films, who died the same year as Bill.)[141]

In retrospect, reviewing Bill's unusual and striking career as one who climbed over one thousand buildings in the United States and Canada and lived to tell about his "Spider" excursions and adventures, the car accident that took his life might just be looked upon as the ultimate irony.

The unbelievable, sad news traveled quickly regarding Strother's death. The *Richmond Times-Dispatch* ran an article that focused on his notoriety as the Human Spider and, more importantly, his beloved portrayal of Santa Claus at the Miller & Rhoads department store in downtown Richmond, Virginia. The newspaper obituary noted:

> *Mr. Strother was in Richmond last December for his familiar role, taking long lists of toy orders from wide-eyed children. He observed then that 1956 children were requesting old stand-byes [sic] like dolls, tricycles and trains, with few asking for space suits or atomic age equipment. He said he believed that bringing the children to see Santa Claus "creates an atmosphere of love in the family."*[142]

The *Richmond News-Leader* also reported the September 7 death of Bill Strother and wrote that "Mr. Strother once worked as a human fly and a stunt man in Hollywood." The obituary read that he used to tell children that "the world needed a Santa Claus who was strong and fearless and could do the unusual."[143]

He did accomplish the unusual, not only as the Human Spider but also as one of the most memorable Santas of all time. People around the country were devastated. Miller & Rhoads was in shock. What would the store do for the upcoming holidays, for which preparations already were in progress? The popular retailer had to regroup and reevaluate the entire Santaland operation at the downtown location in order to best promote its Christmas ideals and hold true the revered traditions that Santa Bill had established and endeared to all whom he touched along the way.

Miller & Rhoads issued a beautiful color image of Santa Bill Strother on the cover of one of its catalogues shortly after his death, along with a tribute. The store honored its promise to continue with the traditions established by Strother that enabled M&R to declare itself many years later to be the place "Where Christmas Is a Legend." The retailer proudly carried on these ideals with its Santaland and the Real Santa and later Legendary Santa until the last Christmas season of 1989 and the final closing of its doors in 1990.

Bill Strother led an extraordinary life and was, in many ways, a man before his time. He would be pleased to know how he enriched the lives of thousands of children with *his* "Santy," as well as how he provided sensational entertainment for adults who witnessed his unbelievable climbs as the Human Spider.

He would probably be disappointed that commercialism in today's retail world has become so extreme, especially during the holiday season. He believed that everyone should recapture the spirit of a more innocent age, when the saying "it is more blessed to give than to receive" perhaps meant more than it does in today's society. He hoped his conviction and dedication would ultimately convey his message of the significance of the true spirit of the season. He believed Christmas should not be taken for granted, and he felt that simple faith and childlike belief are the hallmarks of a celebration that seeks to promote love and charity. In essence, Bill Strother *became* Santa Claus in his heart. His belief in the spirit of St. Nicholas was real and far-reaching. He left an indelible mark on the children of yesteryear, many of whom have become noble adults of today. Indeed, because of his positive approach, kindness and belief in what is right and good, he gave us all a message: to seek, encourage and nurture the hopes and aspirations for the future. The regard for this Santa and his influence probably will never be truly known or even understood. It was a gift.

One thing is for certain. For those of us who knew him as *our* Santa—the Real Santa—we never forgot him and never will. It was *his time*, and we who experienced him are all the better for it. We owe him our deepest gratitude. Because of his gentle manner and compassion, as well as his flair for the fun, fancy and uniqueness in life, he gave us something that we were in awe of and remembered, whether he was climbing a building or being Santa Claus. Bill Strother wished for a better world and contributed to it in so many ways by who he was and how he impacted all those around him in his short life span of sixty-one years.

Christmastime is still a glorious time, but looking back on this extraordinary man and his influence, we see that not just at Christmas but also year round, we have been better prepared to meet an uncertain future,

Miller & Rhoads sincerely regrets the untimely death of William C. Strother, who was killed in an automobile accident in Burbank, California on September 7, 1957. Mr. Strother dedicated the latter years of his life to bringing joy to the lives of thousands of children by appearing as Santa Claus in our store. We will earnestly endeavor during the Christmas season to continue the fine traditions which he established.

Top: Miller & Rhoads honored the memory of Santa Bill Strother with a beautiful color image of him in a store catalogue following his death in 1957. *Carolyn Hood Drudge Private Collection, in loving memory of Frances and Art Hood.*

Left: The Miller & Rhoads' tribute to Santa Bill Strother that appeared with the color image of him in the store's catalogue in 1957. *Carolyn Hood Drudge Private Collection, in loving memory of Frances and Art Hood.*

with our unwavering conviction that he was the Real Santa—and yes, we still believe!

Perhaps there is nothing more to be written to best describe Bill Strother and his special time than the classic editorial that is synonymous with the explanation of who is Santa Claus. Oddly, it was published only a year after Bill's birth, but it is as if it was a prophesy of his appearance on the scene and his purpose in life as he viewed it, as well as how others viewed him.

The editorial, "Yes, Virginia, There Is a Santa Claus," was published on September 21, 1897, in the *Sun* (1833–1950), a New York newspaper. To this day, this piece remains the most reprinted editorial to appear in any newspaper in the English language. And, "Yes, Virginia," it is still appropriate after all these years...

We take pleasure in answering thus prominently the communication below, expressing at the same time our great gratification that its faithful author is numbered among the friends of The Sun:

Dear Editor-
I am 8 years old. Some of my little friends say there is no Santa Claus. Papa says, "If you see it in The Sun, it's so." Please tell me the truth, is there a Santa Claus?
Virginia O'Hanlon

Virginia, your little friends are wrong. They have been affected by the skepticism of a skeptical age. They do not believe except they see. They think that nothing can be which is not comprehensible by their little minds. All minds, Virginia, whether they be men's or children's, are little. In this great universe of ours, man is a mere insect, an ant, in his intellect as compared with the boundless world about him, as measured by the intelligence capable of grasping the whole of truth and knowledge.

Yes, Virginia, there is a Santa Claus. He exists as certainly as love and generosity and devotion exist, and you know that they abound and give to your life its highest beauty and joy. Alas! how dreary would be the world if there were no Santa Claus! It would be as dreary as if there were no Virginias. There would be no childlike faith then, no poetry, no romance to make tolerable this existence. We should have no enjoyment, except in sense and sight. The eternal light with which childhood fills the world would be extinguished.

Not believe in Santa Claus! You might as well not believe in fairies. You might get your papa to hire men to watch in all the chimneys on Christmas eve to catch Santa Claus, but even if you did not see Santa Claus coming down, what would that prove? Nobody sees Santa Claus, but that is no sign that there is no Santa Claus. The most real things in the world are those that neither children nor men can see. Did you ever see fairies dancing on the lawn? Of course not, but that's no proof that they are not there. Nobody can conceive or imagine all the wonders there are unseen and unseeable in the world.

You tear apart the baby's rattle and see what makes the noise inside, but there is a veil covering the unseen world which not the strongest man, nor even the united strength of all the strongest men that ever lived could tear apart. Only faith, poetry, love, romance, can push aside that curtain and view and picture the supernal beauty and glory beyond. Is it all real? Ah, Virginia, in all this world there is nothing else real and abiding.

No Santa Claus! Thank God! he lives and lives forever. A thousand years from now, Virginia, nay 10 times 10,000 years from now, he will continue to make glad the heart of childhood.[144]

ALBUM OF THE REAL SANTA OF MILLER & RHOADS, SANTA BILL STROTHER AND CHILDREN OF YESTERYEAR

The Real Santa at M&R visits with brothers Penn and Scott Burke, sons of store employee Milton Burke, 1949. *Penn Burke Private Collection.*

Top: Judith Harrison (Wrenn) sits prettily on Santa Bill's lap for her Christmas visit with him at Miller & Rhoads in 1950. *Dennis and Judy Wrenn Private Collection.*

Left: Santa Bill and Dianne Dale enjoy a visit together at M&R during Christmas in 1950. *Don Dale Private Collection.*

Top: Sisters Nancy Carolyn Hood (Drudge) and Marilyn Hood (Gunn) enjoy their special visit with the Real Santa at Miller & Rhoads in 1951. *Carolyn Hood Drudge Private Collection, in loving memory of Frances and Art Hood.*

Left: Young lad Wayne Tatum shows his cute clown to the Real Santa during their visit together in Santaland in 1952. *Wayne and Lynne Tatum Private Collection.*

Top: Bill Drumeller discusses
his Christmas wishes with the
Real Santa at M&R in 1952.
Lewis Parks Private Collection.

Left: At Miller & Rhoads
in 1953, Leckie Smithdeal
(Conners) proudly showed her
own "Santa Doll" to the Real
Santa during her visit. *Smithdeal
Family Private Collection.*

Top: Sisters Jane Anne Bray (Wolfe) and Linda Bray (Presson) enjoy their time with Santa Bill Strother at M&R in 1953. *Lyn Presson and Jane Wolfe Private Collection, in loving memory of Jane Anne Bray Wolfe.*

Left: Sisters Katharine Hill (Townsend) (left) and Imogene Hill (Covington) enjoy their special moment with Santa Bill at M&R in 1953. *Imogene Hill Covington and Katharine Hill Townsend Private Collection.*

Top: Brothers Carter (left) and Steve Hudgins from Franklin, Virginia, visit with Santa Bill at Miller & Rhoads in 1953. *Donna and Carter Hudgins Private Collection.*

Left: The Real Santa is visited by a happy little Fred Harris being held by his mom, Freida Harris, in Santaland at M&R in 1954. *Fred M. Harris Private Collection.*

Top: Kathy Moody Brooks proudly shows off her new shoes to Santa Bill during their visit together at the store in 1954. *Katherine Moody Brooks Private Collection. In loving memory of Mr. & Mrs. Sam Moody, III.*

Left: Sisters Karen and Kim Burris happily approach Santa Claus for their visit with him in 1956. *Santa Charlie Private Collection.*

Top: Santa Bill Strother enjoys a sweet visit with his great-niece, Lois Margaret Strother, at M&R in 1956. *Nelson and Marilyn Strother Private Collection.*

Left: Martha Lucas Watts visits with Santa Bill and enjoys a happy moment in Santaland at M&R in 1956. *Martha L. Watts Private Collection.*

Top: Donna Kingery (Hudgins) waves to her parents in Santaland during a visit that she and brother, Chip Kingery, enjoyed with the Real Santa in 1956. *Donna and Carter Hudgins Private Collection.*

Left: Andy (left) and Bill Deekens are greeted by the Real Santa at M&R at Christmas in 1956. *Bill and Donna Strother Deekens Private Collection.*

Top: At M&R in 1956, Santa Bill visited with Blanche Burke's grandsons for an unforgettable moment. *Left to right, standing*: James Sims, Scott Burke, Penn Burke, Bean Walker and David Burke holding Santa. *Sitting, left to right*: Burke Walker and Paul Mennetti. *Penn Burke Private Collection.*

Left: In 1999, Penn Burke's daughter was married and invited Santa Charlie Nuckols (a M&R Santa in the 1980s) to the wedding. Blanche Burke's seven grandsons re-created the 1956 Santa photo. *Penn Burke Private Collection.*

No Santa Claus! Thank God! He lives forever...A thousand years from now, Virginia, nay, ten times ten thousand years from now, he will continue to make glad the heart of childhood.
—*Francis P. Church, "Yes, Virginia, There Is a Santa Claus,"* New York Sun, *September 21, 1897*

Santa's Chair. Original pen-and-ink drawing by Brenton Deekens, 2009.
Brenton Deekens Private Collection.

Notes

Introduction

1. Valentine Davies, *Miracle on 34th Street*, DVD, directed by George Seaton (New York: Twentieth Century Fox, 1947).
2. Interview with Judith Strother Jones, April 26, 2014.
3. Santa Timothy Connaghan, aka "Santa Hollywood," to the author, July 6, 2014.

Chapter 1

4. Marriage license, William Carey Strother and Ethel Grady Weems, February 3, 1923, State of California, County of Orange.
5. Interview with Dan Whitley, May 1, 2014.
6. Nelson and Marilyn Strother to the author, June 17, 2014.
7. Interview with Roger Bynum, May 1, 2014.
8. Stantonsburg Historical Society, *History of Stantonsburg: Circa 1780-2004*, 2nd ed. (Stantonsburg, NC: self-published, 2004), 183.
9. Clifford Dowdey, "The World's Highest Paid Santa Claus," *Saturday Evening Post*, December 22, 1951, 19.
10. "Two Sensational 'Climbers' with Social Ambitions," *Literary Digest* 57 (April 20, 1918): 59.

Chapter 2

11. *The American Heritage Dictionary of the English Language*, 5th ed. (Boston, MA: Houghton Mifflin Harcourt, 2013).
12. Wikipedia, "Buildering," https://www.en.wikipedia.org/wiki/Buildering.
13. Ibid.

Chapter 3

14. Mary Howitt, "The Spider and the Fly," 1829.
15. Interview with Dan Whitley, May 1, 2014.
16. "Two Sensational 'Climbers' Without Social Ambitions," *Literary Digest* 57 (April 20, 1918): 59.
17. Dowdey, "The World's Highest Paid Santa Claus," 19, 69.
18. "Two Sensational 'Climbers' Without Social Ambitions," 61.
19. Ibid.
20. Ibid.
21. Ibid.
22. Annette D'Agostino Lloyd to the author, April 14, 2014.
23. *Concord (NC) Daily Tribune*, January 18, 1918.

Chapter 4

24. *Harrisburg (PA) Evening News*, July 3, 1918.
25. *Harrisburg (PA) Telegraph*, July 6, 1918.
26. *Red Bank (NJ) Register*, September 5, 1918.
27. *Winnipeg (Manitoba) Tribune*, October 21, 1918.
28. How Stuff Works, https://www.history.howstuffworks.com/world-war-i/liberty-loans.htm.
29. *Winston-Salem Journal*, January 9, 1919.
30. *Wichita (KS) Daily Eagle*, July 28, 1919.
31. *Atlanta Constitution*, April 5, 1921.
32. *Augusta (GA) Chronicle*, September 9, 1999.

Chapter 5

33. Michael Futch, "Fayetteville's Human Spider," *Fayetteville (NC) Observer*, December 27, 1998.
34. *Calgary Daily Herald*, September 26, 1921.
35. Harry Sanders to the author, May 27, 2014.
36. *Fayetteville Observer*, "Fayetteville's Human Spider," December 27, 1998.
37. *Winnipeg Tribune*, April 14, 1923.
38. Dr. Donald B. Smith to the author, May 19, 2014.
39. Dr. Donald B. Smith, "The Legend of Chief Buffalo Child Long Lance," *Canadian*, February 14, 1976, 7.

Chapter 6

40. *San Antonio Evening News*, March 17, 1922.
41. *El Paso Herald*, March 25, 1922.
42. Ibid.
43. Ibid., March 31, 1922.
44. John Bengtson, *Silent Visions* (Solana Beach, CA: Santa Monica Press LLC, 2011).
45. Annette D'Agostino Lloyd, *The Harold Lloyd Encyclopedia* (Jefferson, NC: McFarland & Company, Inc., 2004), 308–9.
46. Ibid., 310.
47. Bengtson, *Silent Visions*.
48. Lloyd, *Harold Lloyd Encyclopedia*, 309.
49. Ibid., 346.
50. Ibid., 308.
51. Jeffrey Vance, "Safety Last!, 1923," July 8, 2014, https://www.silentfilm.org/archive/safety-last.
52. Michael Roemer, *Shocked but Connected: Notes on Laughter* (Lanham, MD: Rowman & Littlefield Publishers, Inc., 2012).
53. Lloyd, *Harold Lloyd Encyclopedia*, 314.
54. Ibid.
55. Ibid., 346.
56. Wikipedia, "Safety Last!," https://www.en.wikipedia.org/wiki/Safety_Last!

Chapter 7

57. *History of Stantonsburg,* 183.
58. Marriage license, William Carey Strother and Ethel Grady Weems, February 3, 1923, State of California, County of Orange.
59. *North Adams (MA) Transcript,* November 7, 1952.
60. Dowdey, "The World's Highest Paid Santa Claus," 69.
61. Lloyd, *Harold Lloyd Encyclopedia,* 346.
62. Dowdey, "The World's Highest Paid Santa Claus," 69.
63. *El Paso Evening Post,* February 15, 1928.
64. Dowdey, "The World's Highest Paid Santa Claus," 69.
65. Interview with Dan Whitley, May 1, 2014.
66. Ibid.
67. Dowdey, "The World's Highest Paid Santa Claus," 69.

Chapter 8

68. Ibid.
69. Ibid.
70. Ibid.

Chapter 9

71. Ibid.
72. Ibid.
73. U.S. Census, 1940, U.S. National Archives, in partnership with Archives.com, accessed April 2, 2012.
74. Dowdey, "The World's Highest Paid Santa Claus," 69.

Chapter 10

75. Ibid.
76. Ibid.
77. Phillip L. Wenz to the author, May 30, 2014.

78. Dowdey, "The World's Highest Paid Santa Claus," 69.

79. George Bryson to the author, March 29, 2014.

80. Dowdey, "The World's Highest Paid Santa Claus," 69–70.

81. George Bryson to the author, March 29, 2014.

82. Dowdey, "The World's Highest Paid Santa Claus," 69–70.

83. Ibid.

84. Ibid., 70.

85. Ibid.

86. Ibid.

87. *North Adams (MA) Transcript*, November 7, 1952.

88. *Richmond (VA) Times-Dispatch*, September 9, 1957.

89. Clifford Dowdey, *Virginia Record* 79, no. 12 (December 1957).

90. Earle Dunford and George Bryson, *Under the Clock: The Story of Miller & Rhoads* (Charleston, SC: The History Press, 2008), 27.

91. *Richmond Times-Dispatch*, September 9, 1957.

92. Dunford and Bryson, *Under the Clock*, 67.

93. *Richmond Times-Dispatch*, September 9, 1957.

94. Interview with Linda Scott, April 4, 2014.

95. Interview with Connie Burton, April 8, 2014.

96. Interview with Frances Broaddus-Crutchfield, April 8, 2014.

97. Jane Osborne Johnson to the author, April 24, 2014.

98. Joseph B. Pace to the author, May 6, 2014.

99. Clyde Nordan to the author, June 21, 2014.

100. Dottie Mears to the author, July 4, 2014.

101. Sandra Trott Riddell to the author, July 1, 2014.

102. Bill Deekens to the author, July 4, 2014.

103. Anne Aull Bowbeer, *Felix Adler: King of Clowns* (Clinton, IA: Clinton Printing Co., Inc., 1999), 109.

104. Ibid.

105. Ibid., 112–13.

106. Dowdey, "The World's Highest Paid Santa Claus," 70.

107. Bowbeer, *Felix Adler*, 130.

108. Doug Riddell to the author, May 20, 2014.

109. Interview with Sue Ferrell, June 4, 2014.

110. Ibid.

111. Ibid.

112. Ibid.

113. Donna Strother Deekens, *Christmas at Miller & Rhoads: Memoirs of a Snow Queen* (Charleston, SC: The History Press, 2009), 116–18.

114. Dunford and Bryson, *Under the Clock*, 27.

115. Deekens, *Christmas at Miller & Rhoads*, 118.

116. Interview with Sue Ferrell, July 1, 2014.

117. Dowdey, "The World's Highest Paid Santa Claus," 70.

118. Ibid.

119. Ibid., 69.

120. Interview with Tom Mitchell, April 26, 2014.

121. Dowdey, "The World's Highest Paid Santa Claus," 70.

122. Ibid.

123. Ibid.

124. *Hayward (CA) Daily Review*, May 21, 1951.

125. Dowdey, "The World's Highest Paid Santa Claus," 70.

126. Ibid.

127. Ibid.

128. Ibid.

129. Deekens, *Christmas at Miller & Rhoads*, 15–17.

130. Ibid., 59–60.

131. Cathy Crowell Miller to the author, May 5, 2014.

132. Nancy Bendall Emerson to the author, June 10, 2014.

133. Rick Pearman to the author, May 16, 2014.

134. Janet Pearman Ralston to the author, May 16, 2014.

135. Colleen Covington Simmons to the author, June 30, 2014.

136. Dowdey, *Virginia Record*, 25.

137. Judith Strother Jones to the author, May 15, 2014.

138. Dowdey, *Virginia Record*, 25.

CHAPTER 11

139. Lloyd, *Harold Lloyd Encyclopedia*, 346.

140. Nelson and Marilyn Strother to the author, June 17, 2014.

141. Lloyd, *Harold Lloyd Encyclopedia*, 346.

142. Obituary for Bill Strother, *Richmond Times-Dispatch*, September 9, 1957.

143. Obituary for Bill Strother, *Richmond News-Leader*, September 9, 1957.

144. Francis P. Church, "Yes, Virginia, There Is a Santa Claus," *New York Sun*, September 21, 1897.

ABOUT THE AUTHOR

Donna Strother Deekens is owner and party director of a traveling tea party business, Teapots, Treats & Traditions. A graduate of Westhampton College of the University of Richmond, she has performed professionally as an actress, soloist, entertainer and public speaker. She enjoyed playing the role of a Snow Queen to the Real Santa for many years at the Miller & Rhoads department store in Richmond, Virginia, from 1971 to 1989, and also at Thalhimers, from 1989 to 1991. In addition to her entertainment background, she has held positions in public relations, marketing and fundraising for government, corporate and nonprofit organizations. Most recently, she has enjoyed spending time as a freelance writer. She is the author of three books, *Christmas at Miller & Rhoads: Memoirs of a Snow Queen*, *Santaland: A Miller & Rhoads Christmas* and *Virginia's Legendary Santa Trains* (co-authored with Doug Riddell). She is married to Bill, and they are the proud parents of two grown sons, Brent and Greg, as well as their devoted dog, Missy.